# FTCE Humanities K-12
Teacher Certification Exam

By: Sharon Wynne, M.S
Southern Connecticut State University

XAMonline, INC.
Boston

Copyright © 2008 XAMonline, Inc.

All rights reserved. No part of the material protected by this copyright notice may be reproduced or utilized in any form or by any means, electronic or mechanical, including photocopying, recording or by any information storage and retrievable system, without written permission from the copyright holder.

To obtain permission(s) to use the material from this work for any purpose including workshops or seminars, please submit a written request to:

> XAMonline, Inc.
> 21 Orient Ave.
> Melrose, MA 02176
> Toll Free 1-800-509-4128
> Email: info@xamonline.com
> Web www.xamonline.com
> Fax: 1-781-662-9268

Library of Congress Cataloging-in-Publication Data

Wynne, Sharon A.
    Humanities K-12: Teacher Certification / Sharon A. Wynne. -2nd ed.
    ISBN 978-1-58197-045-6
    1. Humanities K-12.   2. Study Guides.   3. FTCE
    4. Teachers' Certification & Licensure.   5. Careers

Disclaimer:

The opinions expressed in this publication are the sole works of XAMonline and were created independently from the National Education Association, Educational Testing Service, or any State Department of Education, National Evaluation Systems or other testing affiliates.

Between the time of publication and printing, state specific standards as well as testing formats and website information may change that is not included in part or in whole within this product. Sample test questions are developed by XAMonline and reflect similar content as on real tests; however, they are not former tests. XAMonline assembles content that aligns with state standards but makes no claims nor guarantees teacher candidates a passing score. Numerical scores are determined by testing companies such as NES or ETS and then are compared with individual state standards. A passing score varies from state to state.

Printed in the United States of America

FTCE: Humanities K-12
ISBN: 978-1-58197-045-6

TEACHER CERTIFICATION STUDY GUIDE

Table of Contents

Competency / Skill #   **Page.**

1.0 Knowledge of concepts and vocabulary basic to the area of humanities 1

    1.1 Identify the principal formal elements of the arts 1

    1.2 Identify various genres or forms from aural, visual, and literary examples of the arts 1

    1.3 Identify the essential features of various genres of the arts 3

    1.4 Identify significant philosophers and artists throughout history 6

    1.5 Identify the stylistic characteristics of the major art forms of various periods 13

2.0 Knowledge of historical periods and styles 23

    2.1 Identify significant historical events of major periods of Western culture 23

    2.2 Identify dominant philosophical ideas of the major periods of Western culture 25

    2.3 Identify dominant political and economic systems of the major periods of Western culture 26

    2.4 Recognize the influence of non-Western civilizations on the development of Western culture 28

    2.5 Recognize important cultural accomplishments of non-Western civilizations 29

    2.6 Recognize significant Greco-Roman contributions to Western culture 33

    2.7 Recognize significant Judeo-Christian contributions to Western culture 34

    2.8 Relate geography and history to the study of the humanities 35

    2.9 Identify prominent themes of the major art forms of various periods 36

    2.10 Identify prominent genres and forms of art from various periods 39

TEACHER CERTIFICATION STUDY GUIDE

3.0 Knowledge of the interrelatedness of art and ideas 41

    3.1   Identify the effects of historical events on the humanities 41

    3.2   Identify works of art with common themes, symbols, or motifs 42

    3.3   Identify the effects of scientific discoveries and technological advances on the humanities 45

    3.4   Compare and contrast the treatment of an idea or concept in different works 46

    3.5   Recognize the influence of one artistic work upon another 48

    3.6   Relate a major concept to a representative work or person 49

    3.7   Recognize examples of political, social, or religious constraints upon artistic or intellectual freedom 50

4.0 Knowledge of the relationship between a culture's beliefs and values and their expression in the humanities 52

    4.1   Relate artistic styles and techniques to the beliefs and values of selected societies 52

    4.2   Describe how historical and religious forces affect the humanities 53

    4.3   Explain how social, political, and religious forces affect the humanities 54

    4.4   Identify the philosophical or religions bases of significant artistic works 55

    4.5   Recognize how attitudes toward humankind's place in the universe are reflected in the humanities 56

    4.6   Recognize how attitudes toward universal themes are reflected in the humanities 57

    4.6   Recognize how the cultural attitudes toward male and female roles affect the humanities 58

    4.8   Identify works of art that influence the thoughts and actions of a culture 59

5.0 Knowledge of the varied aesthetic principles used by cultures in evaluating art 61

    5.1   Identify vocabulary used in discussing the arts 61

    5.2   Discriminate among aesthetic standards of various eras and cultures 62

    5.3   Trace changes in aesthetic principles 63

	5.4	Recognize effects of aesthetic principles on significant works of art 65
	5.5	Identify examples of Western and non-Western aesthetic principles 67
	5.6	Analyze how perceptions of popular art forms are related to perceptions of traditional art forms 68
	5.7	Justify an aesthetic preference by citing an aesthetic principle 69
6.0	**Knowledge of instructional techniques appropriate to the humanities** 70	
	6.1	Choose effective methods of presentation for various humanities topics 70
	6.2	Select effective teacher strategies for educating students of differing abilities and interests in the humanities 72
	6.3	Select appropriate evaluation methods for assessing and measuring student responses in humanities classes 73
	6.4	Determine appropriate and useful academic and community resources available to humanities students 74

Sample Test 75

Answer Key 96

TEACHER CERTIFICATION STUDY GUIDE

Great Study and Testing Tips!

What to study in order to prepare for the subject assessments is the focus of this study guide but equally important is *how* you study.

You can increase your chances of truly mastering the information by taking some simple, but effective steps.

Study Tips:

1. Some foods aid the learning process. Foods such as milk, nuts, seeds, rice, and oats help your study efforts by releasing natural memory enhancers called CCKs (*cholecystokinin*) composed of *tryptophan*, *choline*, and *phenylalanine*. All of these chemicals enhance the neurotransmitters associated with memory. Before studying, try a light, protein-rich meal of eggs, turkey, and fish. All of these foods release the memory enhancing chemicals. The better the connections, the more you comprehend.

Likewise, before you take a test, stick to a light snack of energy boosting and relaxing foods. A glass of milk, a piece of fruit, or some peanuts all release various memory-boosting chemicals and help you to relax and focus on the subject at hand.

2. Learn to take great notes. A by-product of our modern culture is that we have grown accustomed to getting our information in short doses (i.e. TV news sound bites or USA Today style newspaper articles.)

Consequently, we've subconsciously trained ourselves to assimilate information better in neat little packages. If your notes are scrawled all over the paper, it fragments the flow of the information. Strive for clarity. Newspapers use a standard format to achieve clarity. Your notes can be much clearer through use of proper formatting. A very effective format is called the *"Cornell Method."*

> Take a sheet of loose-leaf lined notebook paper and draw a line all the way down the paper about 1-2" from the left-hand edge.
>
> Draw another line across the width of the paper about 1-2" up from the bottom. Repeat this process on the reverse side of the page.

Look at the highly effective result. You have ample room for notes, a left hand margin for special emphasis items or inserting supplementary data from the textbook, a large area at the bottom for a brief summary, and a little rectangular space for just about anything you want.

TEACHER CERTIFICATION STUDY GUIDE

3. Get the concept then the details. Too often we focus on the details and don't gather an understanding of the concept. However, if you simply memorize only dates, places, or names, you may well miss the whole point of the subject.

A key way to understand things is to put them in your own words. If you are working from a textbook, automatically summarize each paragraph in your mind. If you are outlining text, don't simply copy the author's words.

Rephrase them in your own words. You remember your own thoughts and words much better than someone else's, and subconsciously tend to associate the important details to the core concepts.

4. Ask Why? Pull apart written material paragraph by paragraph and don't forget the captions under the illustrations.

Example: If the heading is "Stream Erosion", flip it around to read "Why do streams erode?" Then answer the questions.

If you train your mind to think in a series of questions and answers, not only will you learn more, but it also helps to lessen the test anxiety because you are used to answering questions.

5. Read for reinforcement and future needs. Even if you only have 10 minutes, put your notes or a book in your hand. Your mind is similar to a computer; you have to input data in order to have it processed. *By reading, you are creating the neural connections for future retrieval.* The more times you read something, the more you reinforce the learning of ideas.

Even if you don't fully understand something on the first pass, *your mind stores much of the material for later recall.*

6. Relax to learn so go into exile. Our bodies respond to an inner clock called biorhythms. Burning the midnight oil works well for some people, but not everyone.

If possible, set aside a particular place to study that is free of distractions. Shut off the television, cell phone, and pager and exile your friends and family during your study period.

If you really are bothered by silence, try background music. Light classical music at a low volume has been shown to aid in concentration over other types. Music that evokes pleasant emotions without lyrics is highly suggested. Try just about anything by Mozart. It relaxes you.

7. **Use arrows not highlighters**. At best, it's difficult to read a page full of yellow, pink, blue, and green streaks. Try staring at a neon sign for a while and you'll soon see that the horde of colors obscure the message.

A quick note, a brief dash of color, an underline, and an arrow pointing to a particular passage is much clearer than a horde of highlighted words.

8. **Budget your study time**. Although you shouldn't ignore any of the material, *allocate your available study time in the same ratio that topics may appear on the test.*

TEACHER CERTIFICATION STUDY GUIDE

Testing Tips:

1. Get smart, play dumb. Don't read anything into the question. Don't make an assumption that the test writer is looking for something else than what is asked. Stick to the question as written and don't read extra things into it.

2. Read the question and all the choices *twice* before answering the question. You may miss something by not carefully reading, and then re-reading both the question and the answers.

If you really don't have a clue as to the right answer, leave it blank on the first time through. Go on to the other questions, as they may provide a clue as to how to answer the skipped questions.

If later on, you still can't answer the skipped ones . . . *Guess.* The only penalty for guessing is that you *might* get it wrong. Only one thing is certain; if you don't put anything down, you will get it wrong!

3. Turn the question into a statement. Look at the way the questions are worded. The syntax of the question usually provides a clue. Does it seem more familiar as a statement rather than as a question? Does it sound strange?

By turning a question into a statement, you may be able to spot if an answer sounds right, and it may also trigger memories of material you have read.

4. Look for hidden clues. It's actually very difficult to compose multiple-foil (choice) questions without giving away part of the answer in the options presented.

In most multiple-choice questions you can often readily eliminate one or two of the potential answers. This leaves you with only two real possibilities and automatically your odds go to Fifty-Fifty for very little work.

5. Trust your instincts. For every fact that you have read, you subconsciously retain something of that knowledge. On questions that you aren't really certain about, go with your basic instincts. **Your first impression on how to answer a question is usually correct.**

6. Mark your answers directly on the test booklet. Don't bother trying to fill in the optical scan sheet on the first pass through the test.

Just be very careful not to miss-mark your answers when you eventually transcribe them to the scan sheet.

7. Watch the clock! You have a set amount of time to answer the questions. Don't get bogged down trying to answer a single question at the expense of 10 questions you can more readily answer.

THIS PAGE BLANK

TEACHER CERTIFICATION STUDY GUIDE

COMPETENCY 1.0   **KNOWLEDGE OF THE VOCABULARY AND CONCEPTS BASIC TO THE HUMANITIES**

SKILL 1.1   **Identify the principal formal elements of the arts.**

In the field of the visual arts, artists utilize the formal elements of line, shape (or form), color and texture to create compositions. The artist arranges these elements according to his/her sensitivity to the various principles of design, such as repetition, variation, rhythm, balance (both symmetrical and asymmetrical), unity, movement (or articulation), and center of interest (or focal area).

In the field of architecture, architects deal with the same fundamental elements as above, but also must consider the aspects of materials, structure, function, repetition, balance, scale, proportion, space and climate.

In the field of music, musicians and composers work with the elements of tone, the characteristics of which are pitch, timbre, duration, and intensity. Musical compositions are created when tones are arranged with regard to rhythm, harmony, structure (both open and closed forms), meter and tempo, texture and tonality.

In the field of dance, dancers and choreographers utilize elements of line, form, movement, energy, time and space. The principles are repetition, variation, rhythm, tempo, narration, space, and setting.

In the field of theater, playwrights utilize the elements of language, structure and theme while actors deal with the elements of language, speech, and motivation. (Set, lighting, and costume designers use the elements of the visual arts.)

SKILL 1.2   **Identify various genres or forms from aural, visual, and literary examples of the arts.**

"Genre", originating from the French for "kind", refers to a style or category of work, characterized by content or artistic style. For example, in the visual arts, various genres include, among others, the content areas of seascape, still lives, portraiture, and religious works. Specific examples for each of these include the following:

seascape- Turner's *The Slave Ship*
still life- Cezanne's *Still Life*
portraiture- Reynold's *Lord Heathfield*
religious- Rembrandt van Riji's *The Three Crosses*

Genres of artistic style include, among others, realism, abstract expressionism, and non-objective compositions. Specific examples for each of these include the following:

realism- Wyeth's *Christina's World*
abstract expressionism- de Kooning's *Woman I*
non-objective painting- Kelly's *Red, Blue, Green*.

In the visual arts, "genre" also refers to a specific style of realistic painting which illustrates scenes of everyday life, an example of which is Kalf's *Still Life*. (See 1.3 and 2.10 for more information.)

In the field of music, various genres include, among others, the forms of cantata, concerto, mass, motet, opera, oratorio, overture, sonata, suite, and symphony. (See 1.3 for more information.)

Examples for each of these include the following:

cantata- Orff's *Carmina Burana*
concerto- Vivaldi's *Concerto for Two Trumpets*
mass- Palestrina's *Veni sponsa Christi*
motet- Gabrieli's *In Ecclesiis*
opera- Mozart's *Marriage of Figaro*
oratorio- Handel's *Messiah*
overture- Mozart's *Cosi Fan Tutte Overture*
sonata- Hayden's *String Quartet in F Major, movements 1,2*
suite- Stravinsky's *The Rite of Spring*
symphony- Beethoven's *Ninth Symphony*.

In the field of literature, a genre is a literary form, such as the novel, the short story, the drama, the epic, the sonnet, the biography, and both formal and informal essays. Other genres include poetry types, such as narrative, lyrical, or dramatic. In addition, works composed in these genres reflect the writing style of the author, and may be classified under headings such as gothic, classic and neo-classic, among others. Works may also be classified by subject matter, such as picaresque, historical, or lyrical. (See 1.3 for more information.) Examples include the following:

historical novel- Tolstoy's *War and Peace*
short story- Faulkner's *A Rose for Emily*
drama- Steinbeck's *Grapes of Wrath*
epic- Eighth Century (?) England's *Beowulf*
sonnet- Petrarch's *Sonnet III ('Twas on the morn when heaven its blessed ray)*
biography- Sandburg's *Abraham Lincoln*
formal essay- Thoreau's *Civil Disobedience*
informal essay- Woolf's *Shakespeare's Sister*

TEACHER CERTIFICATION STUDY GUIDE

SKILL 1.3   Identify the essential features of various genres of the arts.

In the visual arts, one type of genre is based on subject matter, therefore leading to genre headings such as seascape, landscape, still life, portraiture, religious, and interiors, etc. Most of these headings are merely descriptive and self-explanatory. A work of visual art falls into one of these categories merely based on subject content.

Another definition of genre in the field of the visual arts is more specific. A "genre" scene is a realistically portrayed scene that depicts everyday life in a casual, informal, non-monumental way. This type of genre appears throughout the history of art.

Yet another genre in the visual arts is based on the artist's style of work, such as realism, abstraction, impressionism, expressionism, etc. For an example, a painting done by Picasso utilizing the concepts of cubism is said to belong to the cubist genre, while another painting, also by Picasso but reflecting the concepts of neoclassicism, will fall into that genre. (See 1.5 and 2.10 for more information.)

In the fields of music and literature, genre refers to established forms of compositions. Many of these forms have precise definitions and parameters, as given here.

Music

cantata- Developed in the baroque era, these compositions were written for solo and chorus voices, with orchestral accompaniment. With either secular or sacred lyrics, cantatas contain several movements.

concerto- A musical work written for one or more solo instruments with orchestral accompaniment, the concerto usually is comprised of three movements in a fast-slow-fast order.

mass- This choral type is usually associated with the Roman Catholic church service, thus following the form of that service and including six musical parts: the Kyrie Eleison, Gloria in Excelsis Deo, Credo in Unum Deum, Sanctus, Benedictus, and Agnus Dei. Specific masses for the dead are known as "requiem" masses. However, not all masses are written for church services. Since the Medieval period, "concert masses" have been an accepted form of composition.

motet- From the French for "word", a motet is a choral work, utilizing a polyphonic approach. Motets from the thirteenth century were often written for three voices (triplum, motetus, and tenor), and combined texts from both sacred and secular sources. During the fifteenth and sixteenth centuries (Renaissance), the motet expanded to a contrapuntal work for four or five voices a cappella, utilizing a sacred text. The motet also appears in the Baroque and Romantic periods with both orchestral and a cappella variations.

opera- Originating from the Italian word for "work", opera is appropriately named! It is a musical work which, when produced, incorporates many of the other arts as well. Technically, it is a play in which all the dialogue (libretto) is sung, with orchestral accompaniment. The origins of opera were founded in Renaissance Florence by intellectuals reviving Greek and Roman drama. Since then, operatic forms have evolved through many stages. Major ones include "grand opera" or "opera seria", which consists of five acts and is serious in nature, "opera comique", which, regardless of emotional content, has spoken dialogue, "opera buffa" which is the comic opera usually based on farce, and "operetta", also with spoken dialogue and characterized by a light, romantic mood, and popular theme.

oratorio- Developed during the Baroque era, an oratorio is a choral work of large scale, including parts for soloists, chorus and orchestra alike. Themes are usually epic or religious in nature. Although the soloists may take the role of various characters and there may be a plot, an oratorio is usually presented in concert form, without action, costumes or set design.

overture- Usually an overture is the introductory composition to an opera, written to capture the mood of the opera, and even to showcase a musical motif from the opera. However, since in concerts overtures are often performed out-of-context, composers have now begun to write "concert overtures", meant to stand alone, without a larger body of music to follow.

sonata- A sonata is a succession of movements which have loosely related tonalities. The first of these movements usually is composed in a specific pattern, which is known as "sonata form". Sonata form, or sonata-allegro form, follows the pattern of development ABA or AABA, where A is the exposition, B is the development, and the final section of A is the recapitulation.

suite- A musical suite is a group of dances, usually written for keyboards or an ensemble of stringed or wind instruments. The dances are usually unrelated except for a common key.

symphony- Fully refined by the eighteenth century, a symphony is a large scale work composed for a full orchestra. However, the various historic and stylistic periods, in addition to the development of instruments, have produced an evolution of this form. Because of this, "symphony" also refers to compositions for chamber orchestras and string quartets. Although some symphonies vary in the number of movements, in general, the four symphonic movements follow the tempo pattern of fast, slow, moderate, and fast, with a minuet included in the third movement.

Literature

novel- A novel is a fictional narrative of significant length, written in prose and dealing with characters embroiled in a plot Novels are often classified by subject matter, resulting in categories such as:

short story- These fictional works are written in prose, and, due to the limited length, focus on characterization and theme.

drama- This genre refers to a written script upon which a theater performance may be based. Although serious in nature and tone, a drama is usually regarded as a play that is not necessarily a tragedy, and may conclude with a happy ending.

lyric poetry- Deriving it's name from the word "lyre", lyric poetry was originally composed for singing. Generally it is an emotional expression of the poet, subjective in nature and utilizing strong imagery.

sonnet- Refined during the Italian Renaissance by Petrarch, and celebrated by Shakespeare, today a sonnet is fourteen lines of iambic pentameter, a lyric poem that expresses a single idea, theme, or thought, often about love. The many varieties of sonnets stem from the individual styles of well-known writers, thus the categories of Petrarchan, Shakespearean, and Spenserian. Others include Elizabethan, Victorian, and Romantic. The structure of iambic pentameter refers to the accent pattern (alternating stressed and unstressed syllables), and the number of feet in a line or verse (five lines).

epic- This genre of poetry is a long narrative composition, generally documenting traditional heroes and their feats of daring in elevated language. These heroic accomplishments are notable because they have far-reaching ramifications and even significance for the future of the nation or world. The use of symbolism is characteristic in this genre.

biography- Written, factual accounts of people's lives have existed almost as early as writing itself, in as many forms as there are people. Biographies can be as simple as a listing of achievements, or as complex as a psychological analysis. An "autobiography" is written by the author, about himself. A written account of a religious personality or saint is labeled a "hagiography".

essay- An essay is generally a brief, lucid work which presents an author's view on a topic. Factual in nature, essays fall into two groupings: informal or formal. An informal essay is usually short and very personal, reflecting the author's personality and attitude, without necessarily an appeal to logic. A formal essay tends to be longer in length, concisely structured, and more apt to rely on logic and evidence to convince the reader of the worthiness of the opinion.

TEACHER CERTIFICATION STUDY GUIDE

SKILL 1.4 Identify significant artists and philosophers throughout history.

Chronology of Selected Artists and Examples in Western Art

Ancient Greece, circa 800 B.C.- 323 B.C.
Myron: *Discus Thrower (Discobolus)*
Polycleitus: *Lance Bearer (Doryphorus)*
Praxiteles: *Cnidian Aphrodite*

Middle Ages, circa 300 A.D.- 1400 A.D.
Duccio: *Majestas Altarpiece*
Martini: *The Annunciation*
Cimabue: *Madonna Enthroned with Angels and Prophets*
Giotto: *Lamentation; The Meeting of Joachim and Anna*
Lorenzetti: *The Birth of the Virgin*
G.Pisano: *Pulpit of Sant' Andrea*

Early Renaissance, Flanders circa 1400-1500 A.D.
The Limbourg Brothers: *Les Tres Riches Heures du Duc De Berri*
Jan van Eyck: *The Arnolfini Marriage*
Rogier van der Weyden: *The Escorial Deposition*
Hugh van der Goes: *The Adoration of the Shepherds*
Bosch: *The Garden of Earthly Delights*
Durer: *The Four Apostles; The Four Horsemen of the Apocalypse*

Early Renaissance, Italy circa 1300-1495 A.D.
Verrocchio: *David*
Donatello: *David; The Gattamelata*
Ghiberti: *Gates of Paradise* (Bapistry Doors, Florence)
Della Robbia: *Madonna and Child*
Fabriano: *The Adoration of the Magi*
Fra Angelico: *Annunciation*
Fra Lippi: *Adoration*
Botticelli: *Spring (La Primavera); The Birth of Venus*
Ghirlandaio: *Giovanna Tornabuoni*
Masaccio: *The Tribute Money*
Mantegna: *St. James Led to Martyrdom*
Perugino: *Christ Delivering the Keys to St.Peter*
Signorelli: *The Damned Cast into Hell*

High Renaissance, Italy circa 1495-1630 A.D.
Leonardo da Vinci: *Mona Lisa (La Gioconda); The Last Supper*
Michelangelo: *The Pieta; Sistine Ceiling Frescoes*
Raphael: *Madonna with the Goldfinch; The School of Athens*
del Sarto: *Madonna of the Harpies*

Bellini: *Portrait of Doge Loredano*
Giorgione: *Sleeping Venus*
Titian: *Venus of Urbino*; *The Young Englishman*

Mannerism, circa 1510-1570 A.D.
   Bronzino: *Portrait of a Young Man*
   Parmigianino: *Madonna with the Long Neck*
   Tintoretto: *The Last Supper*
   El Greco: *View of Toledo*; *The Burial of Count Orgaz*
   Brueghel the Elder: *The Wedding Dance*

Baroque, circa 1630-1700 A.D.
   Bernini: *Ecstasy of St. Theresa*
   Salvi: *Trevi Fountain, Rome*
   Caravaggio: *Death of the Virgin*; *The Conversion of St. Paul*
   de la Tour: *The Lamentation Over St. Sebastian*
   Gentileschi: *Judith and Maidservant with the Head of Holofernes*
   Velasquez: *Las Meninas*; *Juan de Pareja*
   Rubens: *Assumption of the Virgin*; *Judgment of Paris*
   Poussin: *The Burial of Phocion*
   Lorrain: *The Marriage of Isaac and Rebekah*
   Hals: *Malle Babbe*; *Balthasar Coymans*
   Rembrandt: *The Night Watch*; *Descent from the Cross*
   Vermeer: *Young Woman with a Water Jug*; *Officer and the Laughing Girl*

Rococo, circa 1700-1800 A.D.
   Watteau: *Return from Cythera*; *Giles*
   Boucher: *The Toilet of Venus*; *Venus Consoling Love*
   Chardin: *The Young Governess*; *Grace at Table*
   Canaletto: *The Grand Canal*
   Fragonard: *The Romance of Young Love*; *The Swing*
   Hogarth: *The Rake's Progress series*; *Marriage a la Mode series*
   Gainsborough: *Mrs. Richard Brinsley Sheridan*; *The Honorable Frances Duncombe*
   Reynolds: *Sarah Siddons as the Tragic Muse*
   Copley: *Nathaniel Hurd*
   Stuart: *George Washington*

Early Neoclassicism, circa 1700-1800 A.D.
   David: *The Oath of the Horatii*; *The Death of Socrates*

Neoclassicism, circa 1800-1905 A.D.
   Ingres: *Grande Odalisque*
   Maillol: *Night*; *Mediterranean*

Eclecticism, circa 1800-1900 A.D
    Rodin: *Balzac; The Kiss*

Romanticism, circa 1800-1905 A.D.
    Goya: *Executions of the Third of May, 1808*
    Gericault: *The Raft of the "Medusa"*
    Delacroix: *Liberty Leading the People*
    Constable: *Hampstead Heath with a Rainbow*
    Turner: *The Slave Ship*

Realism, circa 1800-1900 A.D.
    Courbet: *The Studio*
    Manet: *Luncheon on the Grass (Le Dejeuner sur l'herbe)*
    Daumier: *The Third-Class Carriage*
    Eakins: *The Gross Clinic*
    Sargent: *The Daughters of Edward Darley Boit*
    Homer: *Prisoners from the Front*

Impressionism, circa 1800-1900 A.D.
    Manet: *Bar at the Folies-Bergere*
    Monet: *Rouen Cathedral*
    Renoir: *Le Moulin de la Galette; Girl With a Watering Can*
    Degas: *Ballet Rehearsal (Adagio); Viscount Lepic and His Daughters*

Post-impressionism, circa 1800-1900 A.D.
    Seurat: *Sunday Afternoon on the Island of the Grande-Jatte*
    van Gogh: *Starry Night, The Sunflowers*
    Cezanne: *La Montagne Sainte-Victoire*
    Gauguin: *Spirit of the Dead Watching*
    Toulouse-Lautrec: *At the Moulin Rouge*

Fauvism, circa 1900 A.D.
    Matisse: *Red Room (Harmony in Red)*
    Rouault: *Mr.X, The Old King*

Expressionism, circa 1900-1930 A.D.
    Kandinsky: *Improvisation 28*
    Chagall: *Crucifixion*

Cubism, circa 1900-1920 A.D.
    Picasso: *Les Demoiselles d'Avignon*
    Braque: *The Table*
    Leger: *The City; Three Women*
    Duchamp: *Nude Descending a Staircase #2*

Abstract and Non-objective Art, circa 1900-1980 A.D.
    Mondrian: *Composition in Blue, Yellow, and Black*
    Moore: *Recumbent Figure*; *Hill Arches*
    Brancusi: *Bird in Space*; *Mlle. Pogany*
    Calder: *7 Red, 7 Black, 1 White*
    Giacometti: *Man Pointing*
    O'Keeffe: *Horse's Skull on Blue*

Dada and Surrealism, circa 1915-1980 A.D.
    Ernest: *Woman*; *Old Man and Flower*
    Duchamp: *The Bride*
    Klee: *Fish Magic*; *Twittering Machine*
    de Chirico: *The Delights of a Poet*
    Dali: *The Persistence of Memory*
    Miro: *Painting*

Realism, circa 1900-1980 A.D.
    Hopper: *Eleven A.M.*; *House by the Railroad*
    Wood: *American Gothic*
    Wyeth: *Christina's World*; *Helga* series

Abstract Expressionism, circa 1900-1970 A.D.
    De Kooning: *Excavation*; *Woman I*
    Pollock: *Number 1*; *Lucifer*
    Rothko: *Number 10, Four Darks on Red*
    Kline: *Painting 1952*

Pop Art, circa 1950-1980 A.D.
    Lichtenstein: *Whaam!*; *Blam!*
    Oldenburg: *Dual Hamburgers*; *Soft Toilet*
    Johns: *Painted Bronze*; *Three Flags*
    Warhol: *Green Coca Cola Bottles*; *Marilyn*
    Segal: *The Bus Driver*

Conceptual Art, circa 1960-2000 A.D.
    Smithson: *Spiral Jetty*
    Christo: *Running Fence*; *Valley Curtain*

<u>Chronology of Selected Philosophers and Ideas in Western History</u>

Ancient Greece, circa 800 B.C.- circa 323 B.C.

    Anaximander: primary element of life is "Indefinite"; stressed creation/decay cycle; looked for rational, not mythological explanations of the world.

Pythagoras: primary element of life is the abstract concept of numbers; dualism (good vs. evil).

Heraclitus: only change is real; universe is in constant flux; nothing remains unchanged through eternity.

Protagoras: leading Sophist; "Man is the measure of all things"; all things are relative to the needs of man.

Socrates: disagreed with Sophists, believed in enduring principles of morality, to be discovered by the exchange and analysis of opinions (Socratic Method).

Plato: student of Socrates; developed doctrine of Ideas, a spiritual realm in which Good guides the universe; wrote *The Republic*, which outlined ideal society.

Aristotle: student of Plato; had scientific outlook; believed spirit and matter coexist equally; God=Prime Mover; philosophy of the golden mean (all things in moderation); prolific writer on logic, politics, ethics, and science.

Hellenistic Greece, circa 330 B.C.- circa 100 B.C.

Diogenes: leading Cynic; sought after an "honest" man, advocated the natural life and self-sufficiency.

Epicurus: leading Epicurean; stressed good of the individual and freedom of same; denied the spiritual; highest good is tranquility of the mind.

Zeno: founder of Stoicism; stressed good of the individual; denied the spiritual; viewed universe as orderly and good; thus mankind should submit to fate in order to be happy, which was considered the highest good.

Carneades: leading Skeptic; believed that since all knowledge is limited, nothing can be proven; thus good and evil are relative, so judgment must be suspended.

Roman Civilization, circa 480 B.C.- 476 A.D.

Lucretius: Roman Epicurean poet; wrote *On the Nature of Things*; believed in a mechanical universe, with no fear of gods, rewards or punishments.

Cicero: Roman Stoic writer; believed mankind could use reason to overcome pain and suffering; advocated service to the state.

Marcus Aurelius: Roman Stoic; fatalistic in belief that more suffering than good occurred; encouraged people to gain satisfaction from lives lived nobly.

Plotinus: founder of Neoplatonism; exaggerated the spirituality in Plato's theories: emanationism=all things spiritual emanate from God, but matter is without God; highest goal= union with the divine, through subjugation of the body, thus asceticism.

Early Christian Era, circa 350-525 A.D.

St. Augustine: Roman Catholic bishop; theory of redestination; wrote *On the City of God*; advocated the expansion of the Roman Church; viewed the world as war between good and evil; immeasurable influence on medieval thought.

Boethius: preserved much ancient literature in his own writings, including translations of Aristotle's logic; wrote *The Consolation of Philosophy*; highest good= spending life in pursuit of God.

Middle Ages, circa 300-1400 A.D.

Abelard: wrote *Sic et Non (Yes and No)*, a collection of theological controversies, accompanied by writings of clergy that addressed both sides of each issue; applied logic to theology.

St. Thomas Aquinas: wrote *Summaries*, in which Aristotle's methods rationalize basic Christian concepts; emphasized human intellect and reason.

Renaissance, circa 1400-1630 A.D.

Machiavelli: wrote *The Prince*, a description of contemporary practices and policies of government; ascertained that a successful leader put his duty to the state over any and all moral obligations; the "end justifies the means".

Sir Francis Bacon: wrote *Novum Organum*, advocating a complete scientific break from the errors of tradition, and basing science only on empirical knowledge; stressed use of inductive method.

Descartes: rationalist and mathematician; wrote *Discourse on Method* and *Meditations*; began by doubting the existence of all things (sensory input is deceptive), until the recognition that thinking proved his own existence (I think, therefore I am.); dualism= mind and matter.

Enlightenment, circa 1630-1800 A.D.

Locke: political philosopher; wrote *Essay Concerning Human Understanding* and *Two Treatises of Civil Government*; believed people have the right to dissolve government if it becomes tyrannical; advocated natural rights; rejected notion of innate ideas, believed the "blank slate" of the human mind uses sensory data to accumulate knowledge.

Hume: wrote *An Enquiry Concerning Human Understanding*; a skeptic who insisted that it is impossible to be sure of anything; delved into relationships between language and ideas, cause and effect.

Voltaire: author of *Candide*; champion of civil liberties, most famous quote being " I do not agree with a word you say, but I will defend to the death your right to say it."; attacked religious repression.

Montesquieu: wrote *The Spirit of Laws*; believed that human actions are influenced by environment; advocated government of separated and balanced powers.

Eighteenth/Nineteenth Century Philosophers, circa 1750-1900 A.D.

Kant: influential modern philosopher; wrote *The Critique of Pure Reason*; made distinction between "a priori" (independent of experience) and "a posteriori" (derived from experience) knowledge; delved into relationships between time and cause;   believed that individual rights are of higher priority than the good of society as a whole.

Bentham: founder of utilitarianism; advocated social   usefulness, in which all actions are judged on the merit of their consequences, based on producing the greatest good for the greatest number.

Hegel: wrote *Phenomenology of the Spirit*; viewed history and society as evolutionary; theory of thesis antithesis = synthesis; viewed government as a natural organism, only within which mankind could find freedom from social disorder.

Marx: wrote *The Communist Manifesto*; asserted that society has always consisted of the "haves and have-nots" (bourgeoisie and proletariat); eventually the proletariat would gain power, and educate the world into a classless society which would no longer need governments.

Nietzsche: wrote *Thus Spake Zarathustra*; believed that the unimpeded evolution of mankind would result in a species of "supermen", people characterized for their strength, character, and courage. Discouraged religious values because they defended the weak, thus slowing the natural course of evolution.

Twentieth Century Philosophers, circa 1900-2000 A.D.

Croce: wrote *Aesthetic*; distinguished between expression and representation.

Bergson: wrote *Time and Free Will*; distinguished between subjective time and objective time.

Sartre: founder of existentialism; wrote *Being and Nothingness*; believed that the weight of existence and the fundamental freedom of human beings, floundering in a purposeless world, is a source of fear and terror.

Russell: co-founder of Logical Positivism; insisted that it was impossible to know the nature of reality (antimetaphysics); reduced philosophy to a system for problem-solving; developed Theory of Types, an attempt to categorize information more accurately.

Wittgenstein: co-founder of Logical Positivism; delved into the structure of thought and its relationship to language; developed the Picture Theory, which insists that anything expressed in words or pictures relies on other information.

SKILL 1.5 Identify the stylistic characteristics of major art forms of various periods.

Paleolithic/Neolithic Arts, (circa 1,000,000 B.C.-8,000 B.C.)

Although the span of years that separate us from the earliest artists is formidable, those men and women still speak to us eloquently from the far-reaches of prehistory. Paleolithic and Neolithic cave artists were probably community shamans who utilized their paintings and sculptures for religious rituals, specifically sympathetic magic. Their images are predominated by animals and faceless pregnant women, probably rendered for use in fertility rites. The fact that most paintings are located in inaccessible parts of caves leads historians to speculate that the paintings were sacred in some way. Natural materials such as charcoal, stone, and bone are the mediums that have survived to present day. Early artists utilized outcropping of stone to simulate a three-dimensional quality. Since some of the images appear to be renderings of dancing people, historians conclude that dance was also a Paleolithic activity, perhaps used in religious activities.

Remnants of musical instruments, also made from natural materials, indicate that music was also a part of Paleolithic life.

Arts of Mesopotamia and Egypt, (circa 8,000 B.C.-800 B.C.)

Of the two ancient civilizations to span thousands of years along the banks of the Tigris-Euphrates Rivers (Mesopotamia), and the Nile River (Egypt), the older was Mesopotamia.

Due to geographic factors, Mesopotamia was inhabited by a series of cultures from the Sumerians to the Persians. Cylinder seals and vases were decorated with processions of animals and human figures. Sumerians created stylized votive statues with hands clasped in prayer and staring eyes. Temple-like ziggurats served both as shrines to cult statues and as grain warehouses. Inlaid harps and goat figures were decorated with gold and lapis lazuli.

During the Babylonian era, The Epic of Gilgamesh, originally an oral narrative replete with repetition was written.

The Assyrian era was marked by imposing, war-like sculpture and relief work that reflected the chief quality of the society. Lyres, harps, flutes and dulcimers were depicted in the visual arts of the period. Dance appears to have been included in religious ceremonies, most notably in the Fire Festival, a fertility rite.

In Egypt, geographic factors induced a more stable culture whose cultural continuity spanned thousands of years. Egyptian architecture was most notable for the monumental building scale of tombs, temples and pyramids in stone, many decorated inside and out with paintings and reliefs.

Tomb murals, although depicting the realistic life of the deceased, utilized artistic conventions in the portrayal of the human body. Pharaohs were always depicted with divine attributes, with the exception of Pharaoh Amenhotep IV, and Tutankhamun, who apparently insisted on a more realistic rendering. Sarcophagi of painted wood and works in gold and alabaster typify the royal funerary equipment of the period.

The visual arts illustrate the existence of stringed, wind, and percussion musical instruments, as well as "stride" dances used for both funerary and fertility rites. Literature of the period is collectively called the *Book of the Dead* because it consists mainly of prayers, chants and magical information needed by the Ka to traverse to the afterlife.

Arts of Ancient Greece, (800 B.C.-323 B.C).

The earliest artists known to us as specific individuals herald from the days of the ancient Greeks. Following a long sculptural tradition, Myron and Polyclitus produced bronze sculpture in the classical style, which stressed simplicity, dignity, proportion, and appeal to the intellect. Later Praxiteles utilized his famous S-curve (contrapposto) in the marble torsos he produced. The sculptures, many of nude athletes, were idealized, a reflection of the philosophy of the period (see 1.4). From approximately 340 B.C. on, Hellenistic sculpture possessed a more dramatic, narrative quality. Two-dimensional work appears on vases of various styles.

The most notable architecture was created from stone, using post and lintel technique (horizontal blocks laid across vertical supports) to form temples, treasuries, and monuments, also in the classical style. The Classical Orders of Doric, Ionic, and Corinthian were developed. The Doric column was thick, topped with a plain capital, the Ionic column was slender, topped with a volute-carved capital, while the Corinthian column, also slender, terminated in an elaborately carved capital, encrusted with plants and leaves.

Theater, originally associated with the religious festivals of Dionysus, consisted of both tragic and comic plays, also reflecting classical ideals. These heroic tales were performed, with a chorus to provide background and mood, in auditoriums cut into the hillsides.

Arts of Ancient Rome, (480 B.C.-476 A.D.)

Due to the Roman penchant for all things Greek, most early Roman sculpture was copied from Greek originals. When the Romans did develop their unique style, it was, like its creators, solidly grounded in realism. Portraiture was an Etruscan tradition that found its way into Roman sculpture and cameos, also with a naturalistic basis. Most two-dimensional work is found on domestic murals. Roman architecture was practical, utilizing the arch to build structures that could bear more weight, such as aqueducts and coliseums. The classical orders in architecture were also borrowed from the Greeks.

Music was regarded as entertainment and used extensively in society.

Early literature again relied on Greek structure, but writers such as Cicero and Virgil adapted the epic to Roman use.

Byzantine Arts, (610-1453 A.D.)

Much two-dimensional work of the Byzantine era appeared in mosaic form, which tended to produce work of a stylized, impersonal nature. Increasingly, religious subjects were emphasized, leading to the hieratic style, which was an elongated representation of humans in an effort to portray spirituality.

In architecture, the domed church with pendentives (spherical triangles of masonry which couple the square corners of the church with the circular dome), and a cross-in-square floor plan was predominant.

In literature, three genres appear: historiography (written in Greek, following Greek models), hagiography (anecdotes and life accounts of monks and saints), and vernacular poems of fifteen-syllable verse.

Theater seems to have disappeared from the scene.

Early Middle Ages Arts, (300-1300 A.D.)

The early Middle Ages corresponded with the rise of Christianity across Europe. Because the Roman Catholic Church was increasing in wealth and influence, many of the arts found patronage in its expansionism. Two-dimensional art followed local (usually Roman) traditions across Europe, but was generally decorative, narrative and religious in nature. The hieratic elongation found in Byzantine works also made its way to European painting and sculpture. Illuminated manuscripts, crucifixes, cathedral doors and tympanums were all sites for the interpretation of Biblical scenes.

The massive-feeling, dark Romanesque style churches (basilica), with their Roman arches, and small clerestory windows, were springing up across Europe. New musical forms included the hymns, with poetic lyrics set to popular songs, and the Gregorian chant, also called "plainsong", which is marked by a single line of melody, sung in unison, with a single syllable often sung across several notes.

In the field of literature, Christian writers such as St. Augustine, St. Jerome and St. Benedict were predominant. (See 1.4) Secular sources for stories were the wandering troubadours, with their fantastic heroic stories such as the *Song of Roland*. Folk stories such as *Nibelungenlied* were also popular.

Late Middle Ages Arts, (1100-1453 A.D.)

The visual arts began to illustrate a better awareness of space, although the laws of perspective were still to be mastered. Late medieval artists incorporated more movement in their works, and a greater sense of naturalism.

In architecture, the trend was away from Romanesque toward the new building style of Gothic. Gothic cathedrals were noted for the heavenward sweep of the building itself, the height of the roof and spires, the lightness of the interior (due mainly to the increased use of stained glass) and the efficiency of the flying buttresses, which made thin walls possible.

Theater of the day included "mystery" plays, which were essentially Bible stories, "miracle" plays, which were plays about the lives of the saints, and "morality" plays, featuring various sins as characters.

In literature, the influence of the church was still felt, as in Dante's *Divine Comedy*, based on the various levels of heaven, hell and purgatory. Simultaneously, as more people learned to read and write, authors attempted to accommodate them by writing in the vernacular. Petrarch, innovator of the sonnet form, wrote in both Latin and Tuscan Italian. The medieval chronicle, a somewhat fictional account of various people and places, was also a secular genre.

Musical notation was developed, and along with it, polyphony, or music with many harmonious voices. Musical structure became more formalized, and conventions of key, harmony, and rhythm became more consistent. Motets and madrigals were the predominant musical forms (see 1.3).
Early Renaissance Arts, (1300-1495 A.D.)

The Renaissance in Italy produced a myriad of artists who not only rediscovered the classical Greco-Roman arts, but, in an effort to surpass the classical masters, refined various artistic techniques.

Early Renaissance two-dimensional art was characterized by shallow depth, usually depicted by overlapping of objects, symmetrical balance, other-worldly figures, and over-all diffused lighting. Subject matter began to reflect a new intellectual direction, as evidenced by Botticelli's inclusion of mythological characters in his paintings. Masaccio used light (chiaroscuro), perspective, and mathematics in new ways to illuminate human forms and create an illusion of new depth, foreshadowing the High Renaissance.

In the field of architecture, Brunelleschi developed the laws of linear perspective that artists have continued to use. Both he and Alberti reinstated classical proportions in the buildings they designed.

The sculptor Donatello used the classical contrapposto stance in his sculptures but also endowed them with a new sense of humanity and self-awareness.

Writers such as Petrarch and Boccaccio also looked to literary classics for form and ethics, and then emphasized the vernacular in their own works.

In the field of music, the contrapuntal style was developed for sacred motets while the mass was given a polyphonic approach.

High Renaissance Arts, (1495-1527 A.D.)

By the sixteenth century, the pervasive theme in the arts was Humanism. The giants of the age, including da Vinci, Michelangelo and Raphael, made significant strides in achieving psychological awareness through their art. The works of da Vinci achieve this, in part, through his subtle use of "sfumato", while Michelangelo's figures in both paint and marble reflect the humanistic ideals glorifying of the individual.

Architecture also reflected the ideals of humanism as architects, as such Bramante, sought to define the perfect proportions of buildings in relation to the human body.

Music in the high Renaissance continued to develop with the genius of Palestrina, who composed elaborate polyphonic choral pieces for the Catholic Church.

Literary figures such as Machiavelli and Castiglione wrote about political theory and personal conduct, again reflections of humanistic thought.

The Renaissance was not confined to Italy, but spread throughout Europe. In Flanders, van der Weyden, Durer and van Eyck were producing works that incorporated new technologies in engraving and oil painting. The intellectuals Erasmus and More wrote in the Christian humanist vein, believing that mankind had lost sight of the teachings of Jesus, and encouraging a return to more Christian philosophy.

The late Renaissance art in Italy (1515-1630) was characterized by the work of Bronzino and El Greco in a style known as Mannerism. Emotional turmoil, spirituality, and an altered, affected reality were hallmarks of these artists.

Baroque Arts, (1630-1750 A.D.)

Baroque painters across Europe shared similar traits in their works. Italy's Caravaggio, Flander's Rubens and Rembrandt van Rijn used dramatic chiaroscuro (strong lighting) and strong diagonals to illustrate the climax of well-known myths and stories, while their portraiture often gave insight into the minds of their sitters.

Baroque architecture was often ornamental, with emphasis on light and dark, movement, emotion and affluence. The large scale of Baroque building lent a feeling of drama to the architecture, as evidenced by Louis XIV's Palace of Versailles.

Some of the most spectacular Baroque achievements were in the field of music. Opera incorporated the Baroque characteristics of dramatic storytelling and sensational shifts from soft to loud, joy to suffering. Bach's cantatas powerfully express the profound religious faith of the Reformation, usually in a contrapuntal mode for four voices. His music for keyboard, in the form of fugues, also reflects the Baroque penchant for ornamentation, dramatic shifts, and large-scale performance. Oratorios and sonatas also tended toward the dramatic, with an emphasis on contrasting passages and tempos, and instrumental experimentation.

The reign of Elizabeth I ushered in an era of splendor for English literature. Shakespeare's plays focused on the drama of human psychology, dealing with the turbulent and often contradictory emotions experienced in life. In the process, he vastly enriched the English language with original vocabulary and eloquent phrasing. Elsewhere in Europe, lyric poetry and sonnets took on new, more dramatic characteristics, while the novel developed into a more popular, easy-to-read format, as exemplified by Cervantes' *Don Quixote*.

Eighteenth Century, (1700-1800 A.D.)

The eighteenth century spawned several artistic styles, the first of which was an offshoot of Baroque, known as Rococo (rocks and shells), which utilized decorative motifs.

In architecture, it referred generally to a style of interior design featuring a light, delicate feeling, enhanced with curvilinear furniture and gilt tracery, often based on a shell motif. In exterior design, it featured undulating walls, reliance on light and shadow for dramatic effect, and caryatid ornamentation.

In painting, Rococo exuded sentimentality, love of pleasure, and delight in love. Rococo musicians improvised pretty "ornaments" or additions to the musical scores, and composers included delicate and artificial passages in their works.

Simultaneously with rococo, in music a style known as Expressive developed. This style was original and uncomplicated, yet well-proportioned and logical, as evidenced in many works by C.P.E.Bach. Also in music rose the classical style, which was based on classical ideals, not classical models. A highly defined structure, a predominant melody, and an increase in contrasts of rhythm marked the classical style, as evidenced by many of the works by Mozart. Many musical forms such as opera and sonata changed to accommodate these classical requirements. Haydn, Mozart, and Beethoven all composed in their own manner within the classical constraints.

Other painting styles of the eighteenth century included Humanitarianism, the chief characteristic of which was social commentary, and Neo-classicism, the works of which not only detail historical subject matter, but strive to embrace the classical ideals of proportion, harmony, and rationalism. Neo-classicism in architecture reflected the idea that while ancient architectural styles enhance present building, architects are free to mix elements from various periods with their own creative expressions to produce unique architecture, thus producing a kind of eclecticism.

Nineteenth Century, (1800-1900 A.D.)

The Industrial Age brought with it a myriad of changes, as Europe dealt with the ever-quickening pace of modern life. This was mirrored by the multiplicity of styles that surfaced during the century.

Romanticism in the visual arts implied a variety of sub-styles, most of which were characterized by a sense of melancholy, love of nature, emotionalism, and a sense of the exotic. Romanticism was often regarded as a reaction against the cool restraint of neo-classicism.

In music, however, this "rebellion" was not as clear. Romantic music was an extension of classical music, with the emphasis on spontaneous, poignant, and lyrical melodies. Emotion was suggested by rhythmic patterns, key changes, chromaticism and dissonance.

Romantic authors also emphasized love of nature, emotionalism and the exotic and bizarre in their works, as evidenced by Wordsworth, Byron, and Shelley.

Realism in the visual arts, emerging during the second half of the century, referred to both a realistic depiction technically and subject matter derived from a genuine source. As the century progressed, however, the line between realism and romanticism blurred, as romantic artists used realism-style techniques to portray their romantic subject matter more accurately. Realistic authors such as Dickens and Balzac, wrote novels which depict human beings caught in an uncompromising society.

The painting style known as Impressionism was inspired by scientific studies of light and the philosophy that the universe is constantly changing. Artists attempted to capture the transitory aspect of the world by recording a particular moment or "impression", usually working out-of-doors and fairly quickly. Increasingly aware of the plurality of colors in nature, they developed color theories as they sought to record light and atmosphere. Many of the impressionist paintings have a candid quality to them, probably a direct influence of the new medium of photography. Strong diagonals in the composition reflect the influence of Japanese paintings, in vogue in Paris at the time.

Impressionism in music was marked by a refusal to use traditional tonality, resulting in new sounds that composers used to capture different moods. Like impressionistic art, tonal "color" was used, the Oriental five-tone scale was used, and nature was the dominant subject matter. Composers such as Debussy attempted to express the qualities of light.

Post-impressionism in art refers to a collection of personal styles, all inspired in some way by impressionism. The styles were as diverse as the artists, ranging from the emotional intensity of Van Gogh, to the precision of Seurat, to the allegory of Gauguin, to the structural integrity of the "father of modern art", Cezanne.

Twentieth Century, (1900-2000 A.D.)

The twentieth century arts are marked by vastness and diversity. Advances in communication technologies have condensed the world considerably, making cultural exchange an everyday occurrence. Increasing tolerance and interest in new ideas and information result in an even greater stylistic variety. While the following styles occur in the visual arts, some are reflected in the fields of architecture, music, literature, theater, and cinematography.

Expressionism refers to German art, literature and film-making which elicits a specific emotional response from the viewer, mirroring the expression of the artist. Fauvism is closely related to expressionism, marked by bizarre use of color and wild distortion.

Cubism seeks to redefine space in relation to the subject matter and time, usually resulting in a fragmented image. Abstract art begins with a real subject or image, which is then distorted for any number of reasons, depending on the artist.

Non-objective or non-representational art does not begin with subject matter in the real world, and is often the result of the artist experimenting with an artistic/intellectual problem or an aesthetic theory.

Dadaism and Surrealism are related styles that focus on disgust and satire of the arts, and the role of the subconscious in art, respectively. Absurdity, hostility, and the effects of a mechanical universe marked Dadaism during the early years of the century. Surrealism is characterized by intrigue with the intuitive mind. Mimicking the nightmarish quality of dreams by the juxtaposition of bizarre objects, and using a panoramic, hazy backdrop to represent the human "mindscape" were favorite techniques of the surrealist artists.

Abstract expressionism is an umbrella-label for a collection of diverse artistic styles. All, however, are characterized by freedom of the artist from traditional subject matter and techniques, resulting in powerful, highly personal expressions. Pop and Op art, products mostly of the 1950's and 60's, stem from the words "popular" and "optical", respectively. Pop art deals with imagery from popular culture and often carries a message decrying the superficial quality of modern society. Optical art deals with illusionary art, most often utilizing non-representational designs to stimulate eye movement.

Photo-realism, a branch of Pop art, utilizes photographic images in complex ways to convey the messages of the artists. Conceptual art is an intellectual exercise, often using unorthodox materials and requiring the separation of aesthetics and creativity. The idea is basically anti-art in nature, claiming that art is not necessary if the mind is creative. Therefore, art objects can be minimal, temporary, or simply documented.

Twentieth-century music contrasts with prior music in several ways, including the elimination of meter, inclusion of dissonance to a higher degree, and refusal to use traditional tonality. A proliferation of styles marks modern music. Jazz centers around improvised variations on a theme, rendered with an emotional quality that is mimicked by the instruments. Offshoots such as ragtime, blues, swing and bebop, emerged as the century progressed.

In an attempt to control musical elements more tightly in a composition, serialism as a musical style was developed. It involved the creation of the structure of the piece before the actual piece itself.

Aleatory music was an effort in the opposite direction, incorporating randomness in many aspects of the composition. The development of new technologies in instruments and recording has also significantly contributed to the changes in twentieth-century music, although not to changes in style itself.

TEACHER CERTIFICATION STUDY GUIDE

COMPETENCY 2.0   **KNOWLEDGE OF HISTORICAL PERIODS AND STYLES**

SKILL 2.1   **Identify significant historical events of the major periods of Western culture.**

Hint: "Historical" refers to events after the invention of writing, whereas "prehistoric" refers to events before the recording of history.

Ancient Near East Civilizations (circa 3500-800 B.C.)

    c.3500-2500: Irrigation (Mesopotamia & Egypt)
    c.3100   : Egyptian hieroglyphic writing
    c.3000   : Sumerian cuneiform writing
    c.2770   : Early Egyptian pyramids
    c.2000   : *Gilgamesh* recorded
    c.1790   : Code of Hammurabi
    c.1500   : Tempered iron used by Hittites
    c.1500   : Phoenician alphabet
    c.1375   : Monotheism of Pharaoh Akhenaton
    c.1300-1025: Hebrews first occupy Canaan

Greek Civilization (800-323 B.C.)

    c.800   : Greek city-states develop
    c.750   : *Iliad* and *Odyssey* recorded
    582-507   : Pythagoras
    479-404   : Delian League ruled Greece
    431-404   : Peloponnesian Wars
    c.460   : Parthenon built
    427-347   : Plato
    384-322   : Aristotle
    370-310   : Praxiteles
    336-323   : Conquests of Alexander the Great

Roman Civilization (480 B.C.-476 A.D.)

    264-146   : Punic Wars
    70-19 B.C. : Virgil
    46-44 B.C. : Dictatorship of Julius Caesar
    27-14 A.D. : Principate of Augustus Caesar
    c.30 A.D.   : Crucifixion of Jesus of Nazareth
    121-180 : Marcus Aurelius
    380   : Christianity made official religion of Rome
    476   : Last Roman Emperor deposed

Middle Ages (300-1400 A.D.)

800	: Crowning of Charlemagne
c. 750	: *Beowulf* recorded
1066	: Norman Conquest of England
1225-1274	: St. Thomas Aquinas
1305-1337	: Giotto
c. 1310	: Dante writes the *Divine Comedy*
1337-1453	: Hundred Years' War
1347-1350	: Black Death (Bubonic Plague), first wave
c.1450	: Printing press with movable type
1453	: Ottoman Turks capture Constantinople

Renaissance (1400-1630 A.D.)

1350-1550	: Italian Renaissance
1452-1519	: Leonardo da Vinci
1469-1527	: Machiavelli
1497	: Voyage of Vasco da Gama
1501	: Michelangelo,s *David* completed
1509-1547	: Henry VIII of England
1517	: Luther's Ninety-five Theses
1632	: Galileo defends the heliocentric theory
1564-1616	: Shakespeare
1637	: Rene Descartes writes *Discourse on Method*

Age of Enlightenment and Revolution (1630-1800 A.D.)

1650-1750	: Mercantilism at peak
1687	: Newton writes *Mathematical Principles*
1685-1750	: J.S. Bach
1690	: Locke writes *Two Treatises of Government*
c.1700-1790	: Enlightenment movement
1702-1714	: War of Spanish Succession
1751	: Diderot's *Encyclopedia* published
1756-1791	: W.A.Mozart
1759	: Voltaire writes *Candide*
1775-1783	: American Revolutionary War
1789	: French Revolution begins

Nineteenth Century (1800-1900 A.D.)

1804	: Napoleon crowns himself emperor
1807	: Hegel writes *Phenomenology of the Spirit*
1848	: Marx writes *Communist Manifesto*
1854-1856	: Crimean War

1854	: Dickens writes *Hard Times*
1859	: Darwin publishes *Origin of Species*
1870-1900	: Impressionism in art
1876	: Invention of telephone
1898	: Spanish-American War

Twentieth Century (1900-2000 A.D.

1905-1930	: Cubism in art
1905-1910	: Einstein's theory of relativity
1917	: Russian Revolution
1929-1940	: Great Depression in U.S.
1933	: Hitler becomes chancellor of Germany
1943	: Sartre writes *Being and Nothingness*
1945	: First atomic bomb test
1960-1968	: Civil Rights movement in U.S.
1964-1975	: Vietnam War
1991	: Fall of communism in Soviet Union

SKILL 2.2   Identify dominant philosophical ideas of the major periods of Western culture.

(See 1.4 for related information.)

The dominant philosophical ideas during the time of the ancient Greeks included the beliefs that 1) mankind is capable of governing himself without help from the gods or kings, 2) reason is a superior approach to decision-making, as opposed to emotionalism or superstition, and 3) mankind should constantly strive toward perfection.

Many of the dominant philosophical ideas during the Middle Ages emerged from the writings of St. Augustine, bishop of Hippo. Some included the beliefs that 1) the Christian Church has a duty to spread across the world, 2) the Christian Church, like any government, has a right to find and punish heresy, real and incipient, and 3) the use of violence is permissible in converting people to Christianity.

The Renaissance has come to be regarded as an era of tremendous achievements, especially in the fields of the arts and sciences. The predominant philosophy associated with the time was Humanism, the basic tenets of which include the beliefs that 1) classical models of sculpture, architecture, literature, and philosophy in antiquity are not only to be imitated, but surpassed, if possible, 2) it is the power and ability to reason that gives mankind its unique place in the world, and 3) mankind's highest goal should be to acquire "excellence as a person" by achieving a well-rounded education, courage, intelligence, skills in many areas, and action that reflects the worth of the individual.

During the period of the Enlightenment, many "philosophes" dealt with individual rights, and the responsibility of governments to meet the needs of the people. The three premises on which these philosophes constructed their arguments were 1) the universe is governed by natural, decipherable laws, 2) the scientific method of inquiry will eventually yield the answers to questions in all fields, and 3) mankind is capable of learning and improving infinitely.

The ideas of Karl Marx inspired political and social revolutions in Russian and China during the first half of the twentieth century. The predominant ideas behind these revolutions were Marx's thought that 1) social evolution was inevitable and would result in the proletariats of various nations overthrowing the governments. 2) After a process of educating people to the value of working cooperatively, there would be no need for a state government, and it would simply "wither away".

SKILL 2.3 Identify dominant political and economic systems of the major periods of Western culture.

Scholars believe that Paleolithic societies (old stone age) were loosely organized into clans, comprised by a few families living a communal life. The clan or tribe was probably governed by the dominant male or chief, with advice from the tribal shaman, or medicine man, and occasional input from the other males. The economic means consisted of hunting and gathering, a nomadic lifestyle.

The Neolithic revolution, occurring during the new Stone Age, was a shift from food hunting to food producing. Still living in small communal groups, clans began to settle along riverbanks where the stable water supply attracted animals and fish. Eventually these developed into small villages, still governed by chiefs. As the men still wandered far afield to hunt, the women left behind raised the children, planted crops, and domesticated animals, thus sowing the seeds of agriculture. (Some scholars theorize that some societies during this period were matriarchal, with positions of power held by women.)

In the river valley civilization of Mesopotamia (8,000 B.C.-400 B.C.), the villages grew into city-states, each one viewing itself as independent of the others. Because the polytheistic religions were a dominant factor in society, each city-state was a theocracy, governed by religion through a priest-king. Agriculture was the main economic means, although living in cities produced "specialization of labor", enabling people to specialize in specific crafts and thus barter goods and services.

In Egypt (3000 B.C.-100 A.D.), city-states were eventually conquered by a single priest-king (pharaoh), and were assimilated into a kingdom. Agriculture and barter continued to be the major economic means.

In Ancient Greece (800 B.C.-323 B.C.), city-states again asserted their independence. Although most city-states were originally governed by monarchies (kings), Greek idealism enabled many to develop into early forms of limited democracies, in which only male citizens were permitted to vote directly for government leaders. Agriculture, fishing, and trade were staples of Greek economy.

Roman government (780 B.C.-476 A.D.), evolved through many stages. It began as a monarchy, prospered as a republic, in which Roman male citizens voted for representatives, who in turn voted directly for government leaders. Rome was, for a time, a dictatorship, under the reign of Caesar, and later evolved into a principate (empire) under the reign of Augustus. The economic system was based on agriculture and trade.

When the Roman Empire collapsed, government in the Middle Ages reverted back to small local institutions as towns fortified themselves against the onslaught of the barbarians. Trade decreased due to lack of protection on the roads. Feudalism revolved around a local lord, who owned the land but dispersed it among his vassals, who then owed him allegiance and military service. The economy was based on the manorial system, a self-sufficient community, comprised of farmland, villages, and a manor house, which eventually evolved into a fortified castle. Gradually, powerful lords acquired large tracts of land, thus creating kingdoms. The secular feudal system existed alongside the Roman Catholic Church, which, with its own governmental hierarchy and court system, many times dominated the secular government. The Crusades served to weaken feudalism, drawing the Middle Ages to a close. The manorial system crumbled as returning Crusaders gravitated to towns, and the economic system shifted as the middle class began to grow, prospering largely due to commerce, instead of agriculture.

From about 1450 to 1700 A.D., Europe struggled to define itself in terms of nationalism, as kings attempted to free themselves from church restraints. Absolute monarchies, in which monarchs rule without hindrance, were established over Europe based on the premise of the Divine Right of Kings. The economic systems were based largely on agriculture and commerce.

During the years of the Enlightenment, from 1700 to 1800 A.D., radical ideas advocating individual rights emerged. These new philosophies led to revolutions in governments, producing such varieties as constitutional monarchies, in which the power of a ruler is limited by law and other governing branches, democracies, and republics. Economic systems in Europe were based primarily on the theory of merchantilism.

From about 1800 to 1900, the Industrial Revolution changed the face of Europe and the United States. Harnessing power to run machinery to mass-produce goods, countries found their methods of doing business revolutionized and their economies revived. Capitalism, marked by private ownership of businesses and a free market, was the basis of the economy in Great Britain, where the government was a constitutional monarchy.

In 1917, the people of Russia, inspired by Marxist theories, overthrew the monarchy of that country and experimented with communism. In theory, a communist government will eventually fade away, leaving a classless society. However, in practice the government becomes totalitarian in nature, controlling all political, economic, and social aspects of society. As a result, the Soviet Union developed socialism, an economic system in which the production and distribution of all goods are carried out under the auspices of the government instead of private enterprise.

SKILL 2.4 Recognize the influence of non-Western civilizations on the development of Western culture.

(See 2.5 for related information.)

Many non-western societies have contributed to the development of western culture. Representative samples are given below.

> India's many achievements in the fields of language, religion and mathematics have influenced and benefited western civilizations as well. Indian Sanskrit is known as the "mother of all languages". As a result, much vocabulary from Sanskrit can be found in the Romance languages of Latin, Italian, French, and English. Points of view about the world and man's place in it have been borrowed from the Indian religions of Hinduism and Buddhism. In the field of mathematics, the very basic concepts of the decimal system, zero, elementary algebra, and even the form of our modern numerals is derived from Indian culture.

> China's many achievements in the fields of religion and philosophy, technology, poetry and pottery have found their way into western culture as well. Concern for the environment and optimism about the condition of mankind, reflected in the religions of Taoism and the writings of Confucius, have provided western scholars with new viewpoints to consider. Even knowledge of techniques employed in Zen painting serve as a basis for modern Action painting. Chinese advancements in the field of technology have provided western societies with countless inventions, such as paper money, the concept of the printing press, paper, the magnetic compass, and of course, gunpowder. The imagery of Chinese poetry has been enjoyed by many western societies, and has served as inspiration in many fields of art. Chinese calligraphy finds it's counterparts in American modern art, while exquisite Chinese porcelain has been a valued addition in generations of western households. In the 17th and 18th centuries, European craftsmen who were fascinated with Chinese motifs but ignorant of the nuances of Oriental design, developed a style of architecture and decorative arts known as "Chinoiserie", based on designs from Chinese silks, lacquer works, and porcelains.

Japan's influences on western societies include contributions in the fields of landscape design, religion and philosophy, and aesthetic principles. Japanese gardens, designed to represent the harmony between man and nature, have surfaced periodically in western cultures. They have been revered for their simplicity and elegance. The religion of Zen Buddhism has provided new viewpoints for modern western man to consider, as well as the wisdom of traditional methods for meditation. Japanese sensitivity to beauty and good manners has provided new considerations in the western arena of aesthetic appreciation. In the mid 1800's, Japanese wood cuts came into vogue in Paris, where the French Impressionists were inspired by their simplicity, dynamic use of the diagonal, and their sparse compositions.

Moslem cultures, despite growing rifts in religious differences, have contributed to western civilizations, especially in the fields of architecture, education, literature, and medicine. Early Moslem architecture found it's way into the cities of Renaissance Italy, and elements surfaced later in other western architectural styles. Moslem universities acted as preservers and transmitters of Greco-Roman culture, with the added benefit of refining the math and sciences along the way. In the area of literature, fine stories from Moslem countries inspired western authors. Progress in the field of medicine, particularly in diagnostic techniques and surgical procedures, has also advanced health care in western civilizations.

Russia's emphasis on literature, music and dance has benefitted the arts in western societies as well. Achievements in the field of literature have inspired western authors to probe more deeply in their works the ills of western society. Russian music has been enjoyed by generations of western music lovers, while the Russian penchant for ballet has helped set standards for the dance and inspired countless dancers the world over.

SKILL 2.5 Recognize important cultural achievements of non-Western civilizations.

(See 2.4 for related information.)

India

Sanskrit: ancient language of India, one of the oldest in the Indo-European family.

Mohenjo Daro and Harrappa: ancient Indian cities, featuring sewage systems, plumbing, and wide streets.

Hinduism: a complex religion, centering around the belief that through many reincarnations of the soul, man will eventually be united with the universal soul, which assumes the three forms of Brahma (the creator), Vishnu (the preserver) and Siva (the destroyer).

Vedas: four collections of religious writings, the oldest of which is the Rig-Veda, dating back to circa 1500 B.C. and containing hymns of praise. The Sama-Veda is composed of chants, the Yajur-Veda includes sacrificial formulas, and the Atharva-Veda contains charms and magic spells.

Upanishads: a collection of sacred, Hindu verses, dating from circa 400 B.C., stating the relationships between God, mankind, and the universe.

Buddhism: a religion similar to Hinduism, but which rejects the caste system in favor of all men following the "eightfold path" toward spiritual living. Nirvana (spiritual peace), may be reached even in one lifetime by righteous living.

Art and Architecture: based on Hinduism and Buddhism, emphasized ornate design and symbolism, marked by sculptures depicting both humans and animals. A favorite subject for sculpture was Buddha, "the Enlightened One". Temple construction utilized wood, stone and brick buildings with columns, pointed domes and towers.

The *Mahabharata* and the *Ramayana*: epic poems from the ancient period. The *Mahabharata* is often compared with the Homeric legends, although it is approximately seven times the combined length of the *Odyssey* and *Iliad*. The *Ramayana* contains morality stories based on the exploits of the legendary king Rama.

Sakuntala: most well-known work, written in Sanskrit, of Kalidasa, a Hindu poet and playwright of the 5th century A.D., sometimes known as the "Shakespeare of India".

Mathematics: devised concept of zero, decimal system, rudimentary algebra, and modern numerals (misnamed "Arabic" numerals)

China

Teachings of Lao-tse: 6th century B.C. philosopher, taught that since laws cannot improve man's lot, government should be a minimal force in man's life. Man should live passively in harmony with Tao (nature). Wrote book known as *The Tao* virtue.

Writings of Confucius: 5th century B.C. philosopher, noted for his teachings that reflect faith in mankind, he advocated living an active life of learning, participating in government, and devotion to family.

Calligraphy and Paper: decorative writing style using ink and brushes, especially effective with the invention of paper.

Art and Architecture: Art featured ornately decorated vases of clay and bronze. Finely carved jade sculpture and jewelry were produced, while landscape painting was simplified to a few well-placed, expressive brushstrokes. In architecture, a favorite form was the pagoda, a multi-storied temple with roofs that curved up at the edges.

T'ang Poetry: brief poems of only a few lines, filled with imagery from nature, and focusing strictly on a single moment in time. Two master poets were Li Po, and Tu Fu.

T'ang Pottery: clays and minerals were combined to produce a fine porcelain of rich coloring and great delicacy.

Japan

Shintoism: ancient religious beliefs, known as the "Way of the Gods", incorporate nature and ancestor worship with shamanistic practices, such as belief in magic to control nature, heal sickness, and predict the future.

Art and Architecture: influenced by Chinese art and architecture, known for religious paintings and sculpture of Buddha, as well as landscape painting. Some paintings are designed to be used during meditation. In architecture, temples and palaces were set within formal, asymmetrical gardens with well-placed ponds and rocks, symbolizing the harmony of man with nature.

Literature: literature from the "golden age" (794-1185 A.D.) is marked by the diary accounts and novels written by the women of the court, the most well-known one being the *Tale of the Genji*, written by Lady Murasaki Shikibu.

Zen Buddhism: a form of Buddhism which stresses spiritual enlightenment through meditation and discipline of the mind.

Aesthetic Appreciation: marked by sensitivity to nature, beauty, and human relationships, and evidenced by respect for hard work, human dignity, and good manners.

Moslem

Architecture: mosques, palaces, tombs, gates utilized the arch, dome, minarets, and arabesques. Simplicity mixed with grandeur were the keynotes, as evidenced by the buildings of the Taj Mahal and the Alhambra.

Education: founded universities which preserved and transmitted Greco-Roman culture.

Literature: respect for books and learning evident through the acquisition of extensive libraries, most well-known literature includes the *Rubaiyat of Omar Khayyam*, and the *Thousand and One Nights* (*Arabian Nights*).

Medicine: compiled medical textbooks and catalogues of diseases developed the use of anesthetics, progressive in the area of surgery, especially eye operations.

Russia

Literature: field marked by many excellent authors who spoke out on the human condition in Russia, such as:

> Dostoyevski, who chronicled human suffering in his novels, Tolstoi, who denounced warfare, Chekhov, who wrote pessimistic plays reflecting the attitudes of the Russian people, and most recently, Solzhenitsyn, who documented his horrific experiences in a Stalinist labor camp.

Music: field marked by many excellent composers, such as, Tchaikovsky, who wrote numerous ballets and romantic, as well as nationalistic, compositions, Rimski-Korsakov, who wrote operas and other romantic compositions, using Russian folk music as his inspiration, Stravinsky, who is best known for his many ballets composed in the modernist style, and Khatchaturian, who incorporated folk music into his ballets.

Dance: field marked by exceptionally gifted performers, and strict adherence to classical ballet forms and traditional ballet choreography, as evidenced by the performances of *Sleeping Beauty*, and the *Firebird*.

SKILL 2.6 Recognize significant Greco-Roman contributions to Western culture.

Although modern culture is the product of the convergence of many societies and factors, it is difficult to overestimate the importance of contributions made to Western civilization by the ancient Greeks and Romans. In artistic and intellectual realms, the Greeks produced models which were admired, imitated, and, consequently, passed on by the Romans. In the field of architecture, the Classical Orders of Doric, Ionic, and Corinthian were hailed as examples of the most beautiful proportions. Homer's *Iliad* and *Odyssey* served as literary models for countless authors through the centuries. Classical Greek sculpture and the philosophies of Aristotle, among others, were regarded as examples of the highest caliber, and models toward which to strive. The Greek philosophers rationalized a view of the world that transcended superstition, and permitted mankind a more practical, more humane ethic on which to base his relations with others and with his environment. The rational view of the ancient Greeks, in both their religious and political arenas, emphasized particular ideals which are today the basis for modern societies. Secularism, optimism, humanism, and adherence to reason, all coincide to form an attitude that reflects high regard for individual autonomy and human dignity. Advocation of these ideals enabled the Greek city-states to develop governments focused on freedom, as evidenced by the democratic principles of Athens. These ideals have filtered through the centuries, refined into ideals we hold as vital today.

The Romans, although acting as transmitters of Greek culture, filtered the contributions in light of their own experience. Into the field of architecture, the Romans incorporated the qualities of practicality and utilitarianism, producing the like of the aqueduct. Roman literature, as well, was based on Greek example, but was altered to fit the Roman world-view. The Greek ideals of freedom and autonomy found new expression in Roman laws, which, passing into Justinian's code and on into the Middle Ages, eventually formed the basis for the legal systems of modern day Europe. Roman Stoic philosophers (see 1.4) continued the tradition of advocating a free society and recognizing individual human rights, even when the state government failed to do so. The prevailing Greco-Roman contribution is perhaps the belief that it is possible to govern an immense and diverse nation in a democratic fashion.

SKILL 2.7 Recognize significant Judeo-Christian contributions to Western culture.

The fundamental contributions of Judaism and Christianity lie within the realms of the ethical and religious. The ancient Hebrews unwittingly provided the foundation upon which Christianity was built. Specifically, the books of the Hebrew Old Testament served not only as Hebraic history and law accounts, but also as a source of religious law and even political theory for the Christians, who found in its pages religious inspiration and guidance. The Old Testament provided the religious law of the Ten Commandments and the Golden Rule, the basic mythology of how the world and mankind were created, and the traditional view of the relationship between God and mankind. The Hebrew belief system of Judaism is highly significant in that it is the first successful experiment in monotheism. At a time when people feared the wrath of a pantheon of nature gods, Judaism was evolving into an ethical, charitable religion, based on the belief in a single, omnipotent being. In retrospect, the ramifications are staggering. With wide acceptance of a religion based on civil rights, social justice, supremacy of law, and individual worth, society made tremendous gains in the humane treatment of all people.

Jesus of Nazareth, himself a Jew, advocated in his teachings similar principles which later Christians adopted as their own, and which have survived to present day. Among these were the belief in the worth of individuals and the dignity of human labor, the appeal to humans for ethical treatment of each other, and the adherence to the hope that good will somehow overpower evil. After the death of Jesus, the Apostle Paul was left to spread the Christian religion. He did so successfully, in part because the religion held a universal quality, claiming to be the salvation of people from all economic levels. all walks of life, all genders, ages, and nationalities. These ethical views passed on to a large population, forming new attitudes of tolerance and caring than had previously existed, and finding new expressions in the following centuries.

TEACHER CERTIFICATION STUDY GUIDE

SKILL 2.8 Relate geography and history to the study of the humanities.

From the earliest time, mankind and his environment have been explicitly linked. Mankind's survival has always depended on how well he adapts to his environment. From the first person who used an animal skin for added warmth, to modern scientists who adapt new compounds in the creation of medicines, humans have had to creatively use the resources around them to survive.

The study of history is, in essence, the study of how humans relate to and use their environment. The study of humanities concerns itself with how humans express themselves through manipulating their environment.

In the past, geographic factors affected humans by dictating the availability of resources. Whether or not a society developed permanent communities with stable food sources depended on geographic factors such as fertility of the soil and adequate rain. A community fortunate enough to possess a favorable location had time to think, learn, and develop new technologies, whereas another community, with barren soil and little water, struggled simply to survive. Time to create, afforded by an abundance of needed resources, enabled mankind to progress in a myriad of ways.

Furthermore, the kind of resources available also influenced quality of life. In a thousand different ways, from dictating the type of food eaten to the material of clothes worn, geographic factors directly influenced lifestyle. In the arts, this influence is most easily seen by the types of materials used in the creation of articles, and the manner in which these materials have been worked. Societies with an abundance of clay, used it both to write on and build with, and in doing so, developed techniques uniquely fitted to working with clay. On the other hand, societies with an abundance of stone, used it both to write on and build with, and developed stone-working techniques instead of clay-working ones.

Geography influenced societies indirectly as well, as a basis for religion. Tribal shamans prayed to the spirits of the animals they ate and the spirits who brought rain and sun. In later communities, as people attempted to understand the workings of the world around them, ie.-the reason for storms, floods, or a particularly good harvest, they, too, came to view the world as being possessed by spirits of nature. Whether the spirits were benevolent or malevolent depended on the geographic factors at hand. Religions with violent, angry gods, often demanded costly sacrifices to tame the forces of nature, while religions with more benign views were little more than celebrations of nature. These religious views, of course, found expression in the arts and philosophies, and have filtered down through generations to the present day.

Geography has played a major role in the production of world-views held by various societies. Over the years, groups of people, linked by various geographic boundaries, have found themselves sharing similar views of the world.

Sometimes those views are based directly on geographic factors. For example, the isolationist view of the Russian people prior to the reign of Peter the Great, is a consequence of Russia's early physical isolation from Europe. Blocked from communication with Europe by mountain ranges and wide plateaus, culture in Russia followed a more eastern, rather than European, path. When modes of communication with Europe opened, both Russians and Europeans were hesitant to overcome the cultural barriers that had been erected over the centuries. World-views such as these have found expression in the arts, humanities and philosophies across the globe.

Closely associated with the role that geography plays, is the role history plays in the study of the humanities. Like geography, history provides people with a frame of reference, a shared collection of experiences. Those experiences provide a framework for dialogue and expression, a way to arrive at solutions to problems, a way to understand a new point of view. This dialogue takes place between the artist and audience each time a painting is viewed or a story is read, or a musical piece is played. Historical material appears prominently in the arts as subject matter, as evidenced by the many poems written about various battles, and portraits of the "movers and shakers".

At the same time, the influence of history is felt in more subtle ways, as the humanities have traditionally served as a mirror of society, reflecting the events, people, ideas and mores of the passing generations. In this way, the historical artists themselves pass on their biases and viewpoints to audiences of the future. For example, artists today build on the historical foundation of the past. Standard ways of viewing subject matter, such as the conventional approach to nudity in painting, are based on mores that were held by previous generations of artists and audiences. Composers today use traditional formats to organize their musical thoughts.

SKILL 2.9   Identify prominent themes of the major art forms of various l periods.

(See 1.5 and 3.2 for related information.)

The greatest works in art, literature, music, theater, and dance, all mirror universal themes. Universal themes are themes which reflect the human experience, regardless of time period, location, or socio-economic standing. Universal themes tend to fall into broad categories, such as Man vs. Society, Man vs. Himself, Man vs. God, Man vs. Nature, and Good vs. Evil, to name the most obvious. The general themes listed below all fall into one of these broad categories.

Prehistoric Arts, (circa 1,000,000-circa 8,000 B.C)

> Major themes of this vast period appear to center around religious fertility rites and sympathetic magic, consisting of imagery of pregnant animals and faceless, pregnant women.

Mesopotamian Arts, (circa 8,000-400 B.C.)

> The prayer statues and cult deities of the period point to the theme of polytheism in religious worship.

Egyptian Arts, (circa 3,000-100 B.C.)

> The predominance of funerary art from ancient Egypt illustrates the theme of preparation for the afterlife and polytheistic worship. Another dominant theme, reflected by artistic convention, is the divinity of the pharaohs. In architecture, the themes were monumentality and adherence to ritual.

Greek Arts, (800-100 B.C.)

> The sculpture of ancient Greece is replete with human figures, most nude and some draped. Most of these sculptures represent athletes and various gods and goddesses. The predominant theme is that of the ideal human, in both mind and body. In architecture, the theme was scale based on the ideal human proportions.

Roman Arts, (circa 480 B.C.-476 A.D.)

> Judging from Roman arts, the predominant themes of the period deal with the realistic depiction of human beings, and how they relate to Greek classical ideals. The emphasis is on practical realism. Another major theme is the glory in serving the Roman state. In architecture, the theme was rugged practicality mixed with Greek proportions and elements.

Middle Ages Arts, (300-1400 A.D.)

> Although the time span is expansive, the major themes remain relatively constant. Since the Roman Catholic Church was the primary patron of the arts, most work was religious in nature. The purpose of much of the art was to educate. Specific themes varied from the illustration of Bible stories to interpretations of theological allegory, to lives of the saints, to consequences of good and evil. Depictions of the Holy Family were popular. Themes found in secular art and literature centered around chivalric love and warfare. In architecture, the theme was glorification of God, and education of congregation to religious principles.

Renaissance Arts, (circa 1400-1630 A.D.)

Renaissance themes include Christian religious depiction (see Middle Ages), but tend to reflect a renewed interest in all things classical. Specific themes include Greek and Roman mythological and philosophic figures, ancient battles and legends. Dominant themes mirror the philosophic beliefs of Humanism, emphasizing individuality and human reason, such as those of the High Renaissance which center around the psychological attributes of individuals. In architecture, the theme was scale based on human proportions.

Baroque Arts, (1630-1700 A.D.)

The predominant themes found in the arts of the Baroque period include the dramatic climaxes of well-known stories, legends and battles, and the grand spectacle of mythology. Religious themes are found frequently, but it is drama and insight that are emphasized and not the medieval "salvation factor". Baroque artists and authors incorporated various types of characters into their works, careful to include minute details. Portraiture focused on the psychology of the sitters. In architecture, the theme was large scale grandeur and splendor.

Eighteenth Century Arts, (1700-1800 A.D.)

Rococo themes of this century focused on religion, light mythology, portraiture of aristocrats, pleasure and escapism, and occasionally, satire. In architecture, the theme was artifice and gaiety, combined with an organic quality of form. Neo-classic themes centered around examples of virtue and heroism, usually in classical settings, and historical stories. In architecture, classical simplicity and utility of design was regained.

Nineteenth Century Arts, (1800-1900 A.D.)

Romantic themes include human freedom, equality, and civil rights, a love for nature, and a tendency toward the melancholic and mystic. The underlying theme is that the most important discoveries are made within the self, and not in the exterior world. In architecture, the theme was fantasy and whimsy, known as "picturesque". Realistic themes included social awareness, and a focus on society victimizing individuals. The themes behind Impressionism were the constant flux of the universe and the immediacy of the moment. In architecture, the themes were strength, simplicity, and upward thrust as skyscrapers entered the scene.

Twentieth Century Arts, (1900-2000 A.D.)

> Diverse artistic themes of the century reflect a parting with traditional religious values, and a painful awareness of man's inhumanity to man. Themes also illustrate a growing reliance on science, while simultaneously expressing disillusionment with man's failure to adequately control science. A constant theme is the quest for originality and self-expression, while seeking to express the universal in human experience. In architecture, "form follows function".

Skill 2.10   Identify prominent genres and forms of art from various periods.

(See 1.2 for related information.)

Ancient Greek Art, (circa 800-323 B.C.)

> Dominant genres from this period were vase paintings, both black-figure and red-figure, and classical sculpture.

Roman Art, (circa 480 B.C.-476 A.D.)

> Major genres from the Romans include frescoes (murals done in fresh plaster to affix the paint), classical sculpture, funerary art, state propaganda art, and relief work on cameos.

Middle Ages Art, (circa 300-1400 A.D.)

> Significant genres during the Middle Ages include Byzantine mosaics, illuminated manuscripts, ivory relief, altarpieces, cathedral sculpture, and fresco paintings in various styles.

Renaissance Art, (1400-1630 A.D.)

> Important genres from the Renaissance included Florentine fresco painting (mostly religious), High Renaissance painting and sculpture, Northern oil painting, Flemish miniature painting, and Northern printmaking.

Baroque Art, (1630-1700 A.D.)

> Pivotal genres during the Baroque era include Mannerism, Italian Baroque painting and sculpture, Spanish Baroque, Flemish Baroque, and Dutch portraiture. Genre paintings in still-life and landscape appear prominently in this period.

Eighteenth Century Art, (1700-1800 A.D.)

Predominant genres of the century include Rococo painting, portraiture, social satire, Romantic painting, and Neoclassic painting and sculpture.

Nineteenth Century Art, (1800-1900 A.D.)

Important genres include Romantic painting, academic painting and sculpture, landscape painting of many varieties, realistic painting of many varieties, impressionism, and many varieties of post-impressionism.

Twentieth Century Art, (1900-2000 A.D.)
Major genres of the twentieth century include symbolism, art nouveau, fauvism, expressionism, cubism (both analytical and synthetic), futurism, non-objective art, abstract art, surrealism, social realism, constructivism in sculpture, Pop and Op art, and conceptual art.

TEACHER CERTIFICATION STUDY GUIDE

COMPETENCY 3.0   KNOWLEDGE OF THE INTERRELATEDNESS OF ARTS AND IDEAS

SKILL 3.1   Identify the effects of historical events on the humanities.

(See 2.8 for related information.)

The history of the humanities is replete with examples of how history has, in one way or another, influenced various areas of the humanities.

> History provides a common frame of reference (subject matter) in which artists and audiences may express dialogue and viewpoints about various topics. Displeasure over a tyrannical government, for example, may find expression in a play based on a historical incident of tyranny. Therefore, history influences the humanities by providing specific subject matter, as evidenced by the many references to historical characters in great literature, or the many paintings of important events in the history of art.

> History also influences the humanities in a more subtle way. Throughout the centuries, the humanities have served as a mirror, reflecting the ideas, mores, people and events of the passing years. In this way, we gain more than simply subject matter from the past. We also gain the benefit (or liability!) of the experience of our forbearers.

> History also provides the knowledge and foundation, technical and otherwise, for contemporary humanities. Since most of the arts are expressed in some traditional format, historical conventions are bound to play a role, even in the most contemporary of works. In other words, artists do not create in a vacuum. They base their work on a foundation already laid, a foundation reaching far back into the past.

EXAMPLES OF HISTORICAL INFLUENCE ON THE ARTS

> In 1937, Pablo Picasso painted a large mural entitled *Guernica* for the Spanish pavilion in the Paris International Exposition. He chose an allegorical representation to show how the small town of Guernica had been sacrificed by Spanish leader Franco to the brutality of Germany's "blitzkrieg" during the Spanish Civil War. Using distortion and stark colors, Picasso created a personal, and public, symbol for the horrors of war. Although the inspiration, and technique, of the painting, was contemporary, the historical events on which the painting is based, as well as Picasso's moral indictment of the brutality of a totalitarian government, live on in the minds of people who view the painting today.

In 1928, novelist Virginia Woolf wrote a feminist work entitled *A Room of One's Own*. In this piece, Woolf puts forward the views that although the right to vote is an important step in the autonomy of women, equal opportunities for education and life experiences are even more vital. To illustrate the point, she compares experiences in colleges for men with those in colleges for women. Later in the book, she contemplates the various changes in society that the war initiated. In this way, readers today gain insight into some of the views and realities that comprised the gender bias in the early twentieth century.

A study of Roman art clearly shows the preoccupation of the Romans with Greek ideals, even to the point where early Roman artists simply copied sculptures and claimed them as their own. Later, Roman artists and authors created original works based on the format and ideals of the Greeks. Eventually these works evolved into even more original styles. The point is that the Romans served as transmitters of Greek culture, an example of how history influenced the art, not only of the Romans, but of future civilizations who looked to both the Greeks and the Romans for inspiration.

SKILL 3.2 Identify works of art with common themes, symbols, or motifs.

(See 2.9 for related information.)

The field of the humanities is overflowing with examples of works of art that hold in common various themes, motifs, and symbols. Themes, motifs and symbols effortlessly cross the lines between the visual arts, literature, music, theater and dance. Listed below are a few examples culled from the immense heritage of the arts.

Examples of Works that Share Thematic and Symbolic Motifs

A popular symbol or motif of the fifteenth, sixteenth, and seventeenth centuries was David, the heroic second king of the Hebrews. The richness of the stories pertaining to David, and the opportunities for visual interpretation made him a favorite among artists, all of whom cast him in different lights. Donatello's bronze statue of *David* is a classically proportioned nude, portrayed with Goliath's head between his feet. This David is not gloating over his kill, but instead seems to be viewing his own, sensuous body with a Renaissance air of self-awareness. Verrocchio's bronze sculpture of *David*, also with the severed head of Goliath, represents a confident young man, proud of his accomplishment, and seemingly basking in praise. Michelangelo, always original, gives us a universal interpretation of the David theme. Weapon in hand, Michelangelo's marble *David* tenses muscles as he summons up the power to deal with his colossal enemy, symbolizing as he does so, every person or community who has had to do battle against overwhelming odds. Bernini's marble *David*, created as it was during the Baroque era, explodes with energy as it captures forever the most dramatic moment of David's action, the throwing of the stone that kills Goliath. Caravaggio's painting *David and Goliath*, treats the theme in yet another way. Here David is shown as if in the glare of a spotlight, looking with revulsion at the bloodied, grotesque head of Goliath, leaving the viewer to speculate about the reason for disgust. Is David revolted at the ungodliness of Goliath, or is he sickened at his own murderous action?

Symbols related to the David theme include David, Goliath's head, and the stone and slingshot.

Another popular religious motif, especially during the medieval and renaissance periods, was the Annunciation. This event was the announcement by the archangel Gabriel to the Virgin Mary that she would bear a son and name him Jesus. It is also believed that this signified the moment of Incarnation. Anonymous medieval artists treated this theme in altarpieces, murals, and illuminated manuscripts. During the thirteenth century both Nicola and his son, Giovanni, Pisano carved reliefs of the Annunciation theme. Both men included the Annunciation and the Nativity theme into a single panel. Martini's painted rendition of *the Annunciation* owes something to the court etiquette of the day, in the use of the heraldic devises of the symbolic colorings and stilted manner of the Virgin. Della Francesca's fresco of the Annunciation borders on the abstract, with it's simplified gestures and lack of emotion, the ionic column providing a barrier between Gabriel and Mary. Fra Angelico's *Annunciation* is a lyrical painting, combining soft, harmonious coloring with simplicity of form and gesture.

Symbols related to the Annunciation theme are Gabriel, Mary, the dove of the Holy Spirit, the lily, an olive branch, a garden, a basket of wool, a closed book, and various inscriptions.

During the 1800's, a new viewpoint surfaced in Europe. Intellectuals from several countries became painfully aware of the consequences of social conditions and abuses of the day, and set out to expose them. The English social satirist Hogarth created a series of paintings entitled *Marriage a-la-Mode*, which honed in on the absurdity of arranged marriages. Other works by Hogarth explored conditions which led to prostitution, and the poor-house.

In France, Voltaire was working on the play *Candide*, which recounted the misfortunes of a young man while providing biting commentary on the social abuses of the period.

In the field of music, Mozart's *Marriage of Figaro*, based on a play by Beaumarchais, explores the emotion of love as experienced by people from all ages and walks of life. At the same time, it portrays the follies of convention in society.

SKILL 3.3 Identify the effects of scientific discoveries and technological advances on the humanities.

Because the arts and humanities are, generally speaking, a reflection of the intellectual facets of society, they often are among the first to benefit from the cutting edge of revolutionary ideas and technical innovations.

Examples of Scientific and Technological Influences

> For example, when the first European printing press with movable type was invented during the Middle Ages, the arts and humanities underwent immediate change. Many artists switched mediums from painting to engraving, to take advantage of the artistic and economic benefits of producing art to illustrate printed pamphlets and books. With books being mass-produced instead of laboriously hand-printed, the cost of publications was greatly reduced, making books more affordable. Authors, realizing that the audience for literature was expanding, began writing in the vernacular languages of their own countries, a change from the traditional Latin reserved for the educated elite. With discernible books available at affordable costs, more and more people learned to read. As more people learned to read, information and knowledge spread, thus producing an even greater demand for literature and the other humanities.
>
> During the Middle Ages and the early Renaissance, the Catholic Church permitted doctors to dissect one body (usually that of a criminal) each year for educational purposes. Some artists such as Leonardo da Vinci and Michelangelo, under threat of excommunication, found ways to dissect bodies independently. This scientific knowledge had profound effect on their artistic work, enabling them to produce more accurate depictions of the human body and resulting in better control over their means of expression.
>
> During the 1800's, a group of painters known as the Impressionists were experimenting with light and color theories. Scientific studies of light, and newly produced chemical pigments began to replace the ground earth pigments of the past. These synthetic paints opened up new vistas in intensity and color-brilliancy for the artists.
>
> Also during the 1800's new inventions for valve mechanisms in brass instruments, along with standardization in assemblage, produced musical instruments that produced uniform sounds. This enabled musicians to produce music with greater clarity than previously thought possible.

Early twentieth century architecture was changed radically by the production of structural steel, which enabled the construction methods of suspension and cantilevering to be utilized. This resulted in the creation of the International Style of architecture. This contemporary style is characterized by adherence to the basic principles of structure (use of steel and concrete to support tremendous weight), the open plan (decrease the need for interior supports in order to increase space utilization), and functionalism (the concept that a building must be designed to meet a particular function, not a generic one).

SKILL 3.4 Compare and contrast the treatment of an idea or a concept in different works.

(See 3.2 for related information.)

(Hint: "Compare" refers to an analysis of similarities. "Contrast" refers to an analysis of differences.)

 1. As unlikely as it seems, painting during the Baroque period (see 1.4 and 1.5) shared at least two common concepts with Impressionistic paintings created during the late nineteenth century. Both styles of paintings were concerned with the use of light, and both attempted to capture a particular moment in time.

 During the Baroque period, artists such as Caravaggio (in his painting *Calling of St. Matthew*) and Rubens (in his painting *Descent from the Cross*) used light as a vehicle for moving the viewer's eye around the canvas, often in a diagonal movement. Strong lighting, often from a source outside the viewer's range, was used in a "spotlight" technique to dramatize events from well-known stories. Caravaggio and Rubens, as well as other Baroque artists, chose to portray the most dramatic moments from tales, legends and Bible stories in order to convey action and suspense in their paintings.

Impressionist artists such as Monet (in his painting *Rouen Cathedral*) and Renoir (in his painting *Le Moulin de la Galette*)took a more scientific view of light. Due to increased knowledge of the composition of light and how the human eye processes it, they attempted to paint light reflecting off objects, as opposed to simply painting the objects themselves. This approach enabled artists to view light as color, and to experiment with various color combinations. Artists realized that the human eye blends colors which are side by side, and so they painted with obvious brush strokes of complimentary colors. Monet and Renoir, as well as other impressionistic artists, were also influenced by the nineteenth century notion of the universe being in a constant state of flux. As a result, they attempted to paint quick "impressions" of the world, trying to capture particular moments in time before the scene changed in some minute way.

Despite the similarities in these concepts, paintings from both eras contain stylistic differences. Baroque paintings are dramatic, rich with detail, and narrative in nature. Impressionistic works are often soothing and peaceful, devoid of detail and indistinct in form, capturing perhaps beautiful moments in time, but not particularly significant ones.

2. The term "Impressionism", although first used to mockingly describe novel French paintings of the late nineteenth century, also could be used to describe music of the same period with similar characteristics. In Monet's impressionistic painting entitled *The River*, the artist attempted to capture a mood and impression of a moment. Impressionism here is characterized by short, obvious brush strokes of contrasting colors, which the eye blends into harmonious shades at a distance. The forms are hazy, and indistinct, as the artist attempted to paint light reflecting off the object, and not the object itself. Monet was fascinated by the effects of light on water, and strove to duplicate this shimmering effect in his work.

In Debussy's musical composition entitled *La Mer*, the composer conveys a mood very similar to that of Monet's painting, and indeed, is even able to capture the elusive quality of light flickering on the water through the use of high register alternating notes. The discordant sounds, combined with the whole tone scale (C,D,E,F-sharp, G-sharp, A-sharp) used by Debussy is reminiscent of Monet's contrasting colors placed side by side, allowing the ear to blend the dissonant chords to recreate a particular mood.

These two works contrast due to the mediums that create the work. Monet's work is visual in nature, and so captures a moment infinitely in time, while Debussy's work is auditory, and so exists only during a particular time frame.

SKILL 3.5 Recognize the influence of one artistic work upon another.

The history of the humanities is replete with examples of artists in every field, being influenced and inspired by specific works of others. Influence and inspiration continuously cross the lines between the various disciples in the humanities.

Examples of Artistic Works that Influence Another

A) Michelangelo's painting of the Sistine Chapel ceiling (1508-1512) had a profound effect on Raphael, as evidenced by his fresco *The School of Athens* (1509-1511). The influence can be seen by the treatment of the human figures, particularly in the gestures and chiaroscuro.

B) Virgil's epic, the *Aeneid* (29-19) was a source of inspiration to Dante Alighieri, the renowned Florentine writer, who claimed to have memorized the lengthy piece. When Dante wrote *The Divine Comedy* (1308-1321), he included Virgil as his (Dante's) guide through hell and purgatory, a character who represents the highest pinnacle of human reason. In addition, his poetry imitates the form of the *Aeneid* in several places.

C) Dante's *The Divine Comedy* (1308-1321), in turn, served as inspiration for many devotees of the Romantic school in the 1800's. In 1822, the French painter Eugene Delacroix painted a canvas entitled *Dante and Vergil in Hell*, an emotional painting illustrating the anguish of tormented souls drowning in the river Styx, as Dante and Virgil pass over them in a capsizing bark. One of Delacroix's companions read the "Inferno" (the first book of *The Divine Comedy*) to him as he painted. Later, Delacroix claimed that the section that most electrified him was the eighth canto of the "Inferno".

Also during the mid-1800's, the French author, Victor Hugo, wrote a poem entitled *After Reading Dante*, a Romantic piece full of melancholy ruminations. This poem was later used as the basis for a piano program by the Hungarian composer, Franz Liszt(1811-1886).

Inspired by *The Divine Comedy*, and dedicated to the Romantic notion that the arts be related, Liszt went on to write the *Dante Symphony*, reflecting the pathos he found in Dante's work.

D) Homer's <u>Odyssey</u> (c.950-c.800) has, of course, influenced many of the classical writers, but it is surprising to discover that it also influenced the writing of <u>Ulysses</u> (1922) by James Joyce. Because the "stream-of-consciousness" technique is so confusing to readers, Joyce used the classical allusions of the *Odyssey* as a sort of map, to help guide readers through his work.

SKILL 3.6   Relate a major concept to a representative work or person.

Since the humanities deal with the expressions of human thought, there is no shortage of important ideas to choose from. Specific artists, authors, composers, dancers and philosophers throughout history have, through specific works, contributed a multitude of ideas, and new interpretations of traditional ideas, that have changed the way mankind views himself and the world.

Examples of Significant Concepts Associated with Individuals and Works

A) Concept of Cubism in painting, associated with Picasso, particularly in his 1907 canvas *Les Demoiselles d'Avignon*.

B) Concept of Surrealism in painting, associated with Dali, particularly in his 1931 canvas *The Persistence of Memory*.

C) Concept of International Style in architecture, associated with van der Rohe and Johnson in the Seagram Building in New York, built between 1956 and 1958.

D) Concept of Abstract Expressionism in painting, associated with de Kooning, particularly in his 1950-52 canvas *Woman I*.

E) Concept of Humanism in Renaissance literature, associated with Mirandola, particularly in his work entitled *Oration on the Dignity of Man* (1486?), sometimes referred to as the "Manifesto of Humanism".

F) Concept of the Fugue in Baroque music, associated with J.S.Bach, due primarily to his writing of a text entitled *Art of the Fugue*, and to his many fugues, such as *Fugue in D-Minor*.

G) Concept of Communism in political philosophy, associated with Marx and Engels, due primarily to the publication of the *Manifesto of the Communist Party* in 1848.

H) Concept of Impressionism in music, associated with Debussy, particularly in his work entitled *Prelude to the Afternoon of a Faun*.

I) Concept of Absurdism in theater, associated with Sartre, particularly in his 1943 work entitled *Flies*.

J) Concept of ballet on point, associated with Taglioni, particularly in the 1832 ballet entitled *La Sylphide*. Skill 3.7   Site examples of limitations placed upon artistic or intellectual freedom by governmental, social, or religious controls.

Because the humanities deal with expression of human thought, it is perhaps inevitable that at some points in history, powerful forces attempt to repress certain expressions. Censorship, forever a step toward impeding the acquisition of knowledge, has nevertheless played a role in the history of the humanities.

SKILL 3.7 Recognize examples of political, social, or religious constraints upon artistic or intellectual freedom

Examples of Political Constraints on the Arts and Intellectual Freedom

A) In 1830, Charles X of France enacted legislation to censor the press, attempting to force conformity of opinion in matters regarding modernization of France, and liberalism of expression, not to mention governmental policies. The result was revolution.

B) In 1835, King Louise Philippe of France, after an assassination attempt, passed a censorship law which forbade the publication of writings that showed the king in a negative light, as well as the printing of any drawing or symbol without prior approval. The result was increased dissent.

C) After the Russian Revolution of 1917, and during the reign of Stalin (1927-1953), the Communist Party of the Soviet Union conducted "experiments" in the arts and literature, which eventually turned into full-scale suppression of individual expression. The arts, as well as education, were regarded as simply a means to promote the Communist philosophies. Freedom of expression was persecuted, and the approved humanities in the Soviet Union became simply a vehicle for indoctrination of Communist propaganda.

D) During the late 1980's and early 1990's, the U.S. Congress, led by Senator Helms, threatened to withdraw federal grant money from the National Endowment for the Arts, as well as the National Endowment for the Humanities, due primarily to the dispensing of grant money to homosexual artists whose work Senator Helms found offensive.

Examples of Social Constraints on the Arts and Intellectual Freedom

A) After 640 B.C. in Greece, the mighty Spartans imposed numerous restraints on the Messenians, who were enslaved to the Spartans. These restraints eliminated communication with the outside world, due to Spartan fear that ideas of revolt would infiltrate to the Messenians. So overwhelming was the task of maintaining these restraints that the entire Spartan culture evolved into a militaristic society, devoid of any achievement in the arts or humanities.

B) In 399 B.C., the people of Athens condemned Socrates to death, on trumped up charges that he was corrupting youth and introducing new gods. The actual reasons for the sentence included, not only that one of Socrates' former students was the traitor Alcibiades, but that Socrates decried the worship of traditional gods and the disorder of democracy, preferring instead religion based on reason and government based on knowledge.

Examples of Religious Constraints on the Arts and Intellectual Freedom

A) According to Islamic tradition, no images of humans may be portrayed. This resulted in the visual arts consisting of geometric designs of interlacing pattern, animal figures, flower and leaf designs, and even decorative Arabic calligraphy.

B) Between 1751 and 1772, the "philosophe" Diderot edited a series of periodicals, known as the *Encyclopedia*. Diderot's purpose was to examine all beliefs to see whether or not they were rational, with the hopes of eliminating superstition. However, the Roman Catholic Church religiously enforced anti-religion laws pertaining to writing, thus forcing Diderot to couch his philosophy in the guise of humor.

C) During the sixteenth century in Europe, the Roman Catholic Church attempted to turn the tide of the Protestant Reformation by placing strict censorship on artistic and intellectual thought. In 1542, the Roman Inquisition was instituted to rout out and punish heretics, as well as to intimidate people into following Church doctrine. This led to the torturing and burning of incalculable numbers of people for intellectual crimes, such as that of Giordano Bruni. Bruni publicly maintained that, contrary to *Genesis*, other worlds may indeed exist, and for his insolence was burned at the stake in 1600.

D) In 1564, the Council of Trent, instituted by the Catholic Church, published the first of a series of Index of Prohibited Books, which included, in addition to theological essays, many excellent pieces of literature as well as scientific treatises.

(The Index still circulates in revised editions today.)

E) In 1616, the Catholic Church found the heliocentric theory (stating that the earth revolves around the sun) heretical. When Galileo dared to defend the theory in 1632, he was called before the Inquisitors and, under threat of death, was forced to recant his views. Legend has it that, as he left the court, he supposedly murmured "in spite of everything, it still moves."

TEACHER CERTIFICATION STUDY GUIDE

COMPETENCY 4.0   KNOWLEDGE OF THE RELATIONSHIP BETWEEN A CULTURE'S BELIEFS AND VALUES AND THEIR EXPRESSION IN THE HUMANITIES

SKILL 4.1   Relate artistic styles and techniques to the beliefs and values of selected cultures.

Primitive societies, such as the cave painters of western Europe circa 15,000 B.C., are assumed to have held religious views similar to those of voodoo cults today. One of the characteristics of these early religions is the belief in "sympathetic magic", which is the idea that it is possible to capture the essence, or soul, of a person or animal, in order to have control over that creature. Adherence to this belief would explain the existence of the many animal paintings dating back to Paleolithic times. Hungry cave painters may have produced their creations in an effort to control herd migration, or to stimulate the fertility of the herds, or to hold some power over the outcome of the hunt. This would also explain the fact that depictions of humans in Paleolithic art are usually faceless, or, at best, are portrayed with mask-like features. Capturing a realistic likeness of a tribe member would have "flown in the face" of the convention of the time, and would have been taboo for fear of capturing the soul of a friend.

The Classical Age of Greece (480-300 B.C.) produced some of the finest sculpture ever created in the world. The sculptor Phidias produced a colossal figure of the goddess Athena, wrought in gold and ivory, and perfect in every detail. Polyclitus carved the graceful Spear Bearer out of marble, the contraposto of the figure exquisitely executed. Praxiteles chiseled over-sized, sensual Aphrodite, with serene expressions and a sense of order. All of these artists aspired to produce works that reflected the ideals of Greek society at the time, the ideals of perfection, strength, grace and freedom. Greek artists created works that emulated the ideal human being, the supreme goal the Greeks believed all men and women should strive toward. Ideal traits included perfection in mind and body, both physical strength and strength of character, and grace in all things. Freedom was a goal believed attainable by the Greeks, due to their military successes against the mighty Persian Empire (490-480 B.C.). Even Greek religion invited love of freedom, since this polytheistic religion was without dogma or commandments, and humans were thought to be intelligent enough to bargain with the gods. It is little wonder, then, that a society with such an optimistic view of it's members should produce art so full of idealism, and it is of no wonder that such a society should be emulated and imitated so often throughout history.

Most religions have, at one time or another mandated certain conventions on art affiliated with the organization. Islamic art, for example, contains no human imagery, due to religious laws that forbid image worship. Byzantine religious art, on the other hand, is composed almost exclusively of icons, religious portraits that are believed useful in focusing prayer more directly toward heaven. Ancient Egyptian pharaoh worship demanded that renderings of the pharaohs portray them only as flawless, unemotional divinities. Christianity during the Middle Ages emphasized the suffering of Jesus on the cross and the accompanying guilt of the parishioners, thus producing art that graphically depicted the horrors of crucifixion and the torture chamber that was hell.

SKILL 4.2 Describe how historical and religious events are portrayed by selected cultures.

Preliterate societies probably passed religious and historical information on from one generation to the next, by using mnemonic exercises as part of initiation rites and religious rituals. Group memories of important tribal events were the domain of the community storytellers, and were transmitted from one generation to the next through the use of long poems and chants set to music. It is likely that dance was also enlisted to communicate tribal history and insure it's continuity in the tribe's traditions.

Ancient cultures relied on oral epic poems and mythologies from the past on which to base their traditions. Often the historical information was couched in religious terms, as in the Sumerian mythologies in which warring gods and goddesses actually portrayed feuding city-states. Eventually these orally transmitted stories were written down, forming the basis for the mythologies and legends we know today.

"To the victors go the spoils", and so, apparently, do the publishing rights. The winners in any war gain the privilege of having history viewed through their eyes, and usually their eyes alone. The Romans were masters at propaganda, and enlisted the aid of many historians and other writers to create history books favorable to the Roman perspective. They also wrote Roman mythologies that "altered" the past in order to help the new Roman conquerors gain respectability with their new subjects.

During the Medieval period, the Roman Catholic Church served as both religious institution and government. Since there was no real separation of church and state, portrayals of religious events and historical events tended to mesh together, as evidenced by the many church paintings depicting both historical characters and contemporary people in religious settings. Religious law became state law, and religious truths were assumed to be the truths that all people, regardless of personal beliefs, must adhere to. Because the Church collected taxes, it had money to construct buildings which served both church and municipal functions. The churches were filled with religious art, depicting stories which were accepted as historically-accurate fact.

SKILL 4.3 Explain how social, political, and religious forces affect the humanities.

It is often said that the arts are a mirror of society, reflecting the morals, attitudes and concerns of people in any given culture. Because the humanities deal with the expression of the human experience, it stands to reason that society's views of what is appropriate to reveal about that experience plays a major role in what artists express. At any time in history, political, social, and religious powers have influenced what artists feel comfortable expressing.

(In contrast to this is the view of "art for art's sake", a slogan touted by Oscar Wilde and Samuel Coleridge, among others. This opinion holds that the arts, out of necessity, are outside the realm of these forces, and that art can and should exist solely for its own benefit and because of its intrinsic beauty.)

Political influence can be seen in the monumental sculpture of the Roman Empire, constructed to glorify the state. An example is the 6'8" sculpture of *Augustus in Armor*, depicting the emperor as a consul, confidently striding forward to deliver an inspiring speech to his legions. The bare feet denote courage, while the staff symbolizes the power of the emperor over the Roman Senate. The bronze *Equestrian Statue of Marcus Aurelius* serves as a second example, illustrating the "philosopher-king" concept of the emperor as a man of learning, ruling over Rome with wisdom and justice instead of brute force.

A recent example of how governmental powers affect the humanities can be viewed in the early twentieth-century in the Soviet Union. The communist regime feared artists might encourage the onset of capitalism and democracy, and accordingly took actions to repress freedom of expression in favor of rhetoric favorable to the cause of communism, including persecution of artists and authors. The result was an outpouring of state-produced, stilted graphic art and literature, while meaningful expressions in the arts had to be smuggled out of the country to receive acclaim. Aleksandr Solzhenitsyn, author of *One Day in the Life of Ivan Denisovich* and *The Gulag Archipelago*, was forced to live in exile for several years.

C) The influence of religion on art can most clearly be viewed in the works of the medieval European period. During this era, the Roman Catholic Church ruled as a state government, and, as such, was the major patron of the arts. As a result, much of the art from this period was religious in nature. Examples are Duccio's *Christ Entering Jerusalem* and Master Honore's *David and Goliath*.

SKILL 4.4 Identify the philosophical or religious bases of significant artistic works.

Winged Victory of Samothrace, c.200-190 B.C.
    This Hellenistic sculpture depicts the legend in which Nike, the goddess of war, alighted on the prow of an Athenian trieme to lead the Greeks to victory against the Persians during the Battle of Salamis. The sculpture is founded on the Greek concept of beauty, in which ideal human proportions meld with the powers of human reasoning, an ideology which coincides with that of Plato. This sculpture is considered to be the greatest of the Hellenistic works due to the interdependency of the mass and the space around it, again a reflection of the relationship between the physical and the intangible.

The Gero Crucifix, c.975-1000 A.D.
    This Ottonian sculpture, depicting the crucifixion of Jesus, was created for the Cathedral of Cologne during the reign of Otto II, a time of artistic supremacy in Germany. The religious basis for the work is the Christian belief that the crucifixion and death of Jesus was necessary for the savior to redeem Christian souls to heaven. This belief is reflected in the "expressive realism" of the crucifix. The forward thrust of the body gives the illusion of heavy weight, which seems to strain tortuously on the arms and shoulders of the figure. This painful rendition of the death of Jesus is calculated to elicit feelings of sympathy and guilt from the viewer.

School of Athens by Raphael, 1510-11 A.D.
    This Renaissance fresco depicts famous Greek philosophers (modeled after Renaissance celebrities) grouped around Plato and Aristotle, each engaged in a characteristic activity. With his finger pointing to the heavens, Plato, and the figures on his side of the composition, represents "idealism". Aristotle, with his hand reaching to touch the earth, leads the opposing figures to represent "realism". This fresco is considered to be the embodiment of the classic spirit (idealism and realism) which manifested during the Italian Renaissance.

Demoiselles d'Avignon by Picasso, 1906-7 A.D.
    This cubist abstraction, depicting five nudes, is a significant modern work, due to the landmark quality of it's visual theories. Broken into shaded angular facets which give the illusion of three-dimensionality, the features of the nudes are viewed from various angles simultaneously. The philosophical basis is a "splintered view" of the world, one in which surface appearances are deceiving, due to the complexities of nature and the multi-faceted nature of reality. Because the universe is in constant flux, everything is in a state of transition, and nothing remains constant.

SKILL 4.5 Recognize how attitudes toward humankind's place in the universe are reflected in the humanities.

(See related information in 1.4 and 2.2.)

One of the most human experiences is to wonder why we exist, and what our role in the universe really is. The humanity, in seeking to define or express the human experience, by necessity addresses the various viewpoints to this riddle. From Paleolithic cave paintings to the abstractions of modern expression, arts and humanities reflect this dilemma. Consciously and unconsciously, by the expressions in the works, and by the methods of working, artists, authors and philosophers all contribute to the sum of what humans think or believe about our role in the universe.

Ancient Greeks were avid believers in democracy and liberty, even to the point that their religion was based on the premise that gods and mankind could co-exist to each other's mutual benefit. This belief was reflected in the architecture of Greek temples, an architecture based on human proportions and the "Golden Mean". The world was thought to be a rational place where reasoning men could govern themselves without fear of an angry, vengeful god. This ideal of the perfect, rational human continued to manifest itself in the sculpture and philosophy of the day, as evidenced by classic and Hellenic sculpture, and by the works of Plato, among others.

By comparison, medieval European scholars were trained by the Roman Catholic Church in theology and Church doctrine. Their views of mankind's role in the universe were colored by religious attitudes, and, because these educated people were in positions of power, everyone was forced to concede to the same philosophy, or face charges of blasphemy. Everything in the arts, from Church architecture to music to sculpture to manuscript illustration, was designed to teach the illiterate masses about the rules and doctrine of the Roman Catholic Church. Churches were constructed in the shape of crosses, stained glass windows reflected Bible stories and images of saints, and mosaics illustrated the terrors of Hell. Mankind was thought to be at the service of God, and the solidity of Romanesque architecture and the soaring spires of Gothic churches reinforced the belief that God was ultimate while man was a sinful, depraved creature. Art works remained anonymous as further proof that the glory of God was not to be overshadowed by any accomplishment of mankind.

During the Renaissance, the classic philosophy (idealism and realism) of the Greeks and Romans was rediscovered, and ushered in a new era of rationalism and humanism. Spectacular new art works by Leonardo da Vinci, Michelangelo, and Raphael surpassed anything the world had ever seen. These works not only glorified God, but earned the highest respect for the artists who created them. Architecture returned to proportions based on human anatomy, but the real effects were most clearly felt in the fields of literature, philosophy, and religion.

The development of Gutenburg's printing press resulted in increased availability of printed material. As more people learned to read, literature led the new wave of intellectualism. Philosophical writings about mankind's place in the universe, such as Mirandola's *Oration on the Dignity of Man*, and pamphlets by Luther, increased in circulation, bringing with them the ire of the Roman Catholic Church, the beginnings of the Inquisition, and an outpouring of new religious, protestant faiths. Movements such as the Reformation and Counter-reformation, which would have been unthinkable during the medieval period, were inevitable with the resurgence of humanism.

Jean-Paul Sartre, a twentieth century French author and philosopher, is credited with the development of Existentialism, a philosophy which questions the nature of human existence. The philosophy contends that because human history is filled with cruelty, humans are filled with guilt. Human quest for freedom leads only to terror, therefore human existence is ultimately meaningless. This philosophy led to other developments in the arts and humanities, most notably in the field of theater, where Satre also contributed plays in the so-called "absurdist style".

Plays such as *Flies*, and *No Exit* placed the Existential philosophy before the public.

Early Dadaists, such as George Grosz, also drew on existential thought while designing some of their early experimental works. Later conceptual artists also relied on existential themes while choreographing "happenings" during the 1960's and early 70's.

SKILL 4.6   Recognize how attitudes toward universal themes are reflected in the humanities.

Each artist and author brings to his/her work his own personal view of the world, based on his own experiences. Those of us who view the works and read the books also bring our own biases to the experience. Therefore, the universal themes that are reflected in artistic works are colored both by the hands that create the works and the eyes that perceive them. Is it any wonder, then, that every work in the arts and humanities is open to so many varied interpretations?

Universal themes are themes that reflect the human experience, regardless of time period, location, social standing or economic considerations, religious or cultural beliefs. However, individuals or societies may condone or object to the particular manner in which a theme is approached.

For example, during the Renaissance, Michelangelo painted the ceiling of the Sistine Chapel with glowing frescoes, the theme of which is the creation of the universe and man. Although the frescoes are based on stories from the Old Testament, the theme is universal in that mankind has always sought to understand his origins. During Michelangelo's own time, controversy surrounded the ceiling frescoes, due in large measure to the manner in which Michelangelo portrayed the theme. Church scholars were divided over whether Michelangelo had departed too far from the classical notions of beauty advocated by the ancient Greeks, or whether he had followed the Greek conventions (including nudity) too closely! Michelangelo contended that his style was a personal one, derived in part from observation of classical sculpture, and in part from his observations from life. He expressed a desire to paint differently from the Greeks, because the society he was painting for was dramatically different from the Greek society.

The most obvious way in which attitudes toward universal themes are reflected in the humanities is the ability of the artist to express his opinions through his work. For example, the English satirist, William Hogarth, addressed the universal themes of social cruelty through his paintings. Because of his dramatic portrayals and biting satire, Hogarth's works reflect his own humanitarian viewpoints regarding his 18th century English society. The fact that his paintings aroused similar emotions among the general public is evidenced by the fact that his series of paintings were made into engravings, so that they would be more affordable to the masses of people who sought to buy them. The wide distribution of these prints indicates the extent to which the public sought social change.

SKILL 4.7 Recognize how the cultural attitudes toward male and female roles affect the humanities.

Cultural attitudes toward the roles of males and females in society affect the humanities in at least two areas, as topics for expression, and as stereotypes regarding the abilities of artists and authors.

Cultural attitudes toward gender roles provide rich fodder for expression in the arts. Over the centuries, artists have, both wittingly and not, documented the roles of women and children in predominantly patriarchal societies. Examples include Egyptian tomb paintings, Greek vase paintings, and Roman murals illustrating the roles women played in those societies. The religious art of the medieval and Renaissance periods implies a sort of schizophrenia in the traditional view of the Catholic Church toward women. On one hand, Mary is portrayed as the role model toward which all women are suppose to aspire, while at the same time, women were generally associated, and blamed, with the expulsion of Adam from the Garden of Eden.

In the field of literature, many authors have drawn on cultural attitudes toward gender roles as material for their works. Examples include Virginia Woolf's observations that, because of attitudes concerning the role of women in society, a female writer during the time of Shakespeare could never have had access to the same opportunities that resulted in Shakespeare's works gaining such notoriety. Oscar Wilde also wrote about gender differences, but took an opposing point of view.

Dance is an interesting indicator of gender roles in society. Various cultures have, at different times, forbidden one sex or the other to participate in dance. Primitive dances were designed for specific functions, such as fertility rites (women) or hunting dances (men), to be used only by a selected group of individuals whose gender role in society necessitated the dance. Later in history, as in Renaissance Italy, only men were permitted to dance, although they occasionally danced female roles.

Cultural attitudes toward gender roles can manifest themselves in stereotypes regarding the abilities of artists and authors. In less enlightened times or locations, cultural biases have lead to the creation of stereotypes regarding the abilities of one gender or another in regard to artistic abilities. Primitive societies often forbade women to engage in creative activities in the area of visual art. Medieval societies often repressed women in the fields of learning, which resulted in few women authors producing anything of note.

SKILL 4.8   Identify works of art that influence thoughts and actions of a culture.

Not only are the arts and humanities a mirror of society, reflecting the morals and attitudes of people, but they also serve society by communicating messages and ideas. Occasionally, an artistic work or piece of literature will so touch the hearts and minds of people that it will serve as a rallying point for opinions, and even actions. Examples follow.

A) The field of literature holds many examples of works that influence opinion and incite people to action. One of the most obvious is also one of the oldest collections of stories and poetry compiled, *The Bible*. Serving as the basis and/or inspiration for several religions, these writings have spawned countless beliefs, morals, wars, and acts of benevolence. Another example from ancient history is Plato's Dialogues. A cornerstone of philosophic thought, philosophers through the centuries have referred back to this writing to prove or disprove new theories. From the Renaissance period, Dante's The *Divine Comedy* portrayed the afterlife in a fashion that colored Christian beliefs ever since. Artists and composers, inspired by Dante's vision, have created works based on this masterpiece. Machiavelli's *The Prince* was written as a guide for rulers, and has doubtless served as justification for many an unscrupulous action. In a more recent vein, the poetry of Langston Hughes, such as *Harlem,* served as food for thought for the 1960's and 70's generation of college students, leading to many campus demonstrations during the civil rights movement.

B) Architecture has a subtle way of influencing the minds of people. Use of space, lighting, color and texture work together to create environments that influence people without their notice. History is replete with architectural examples that reinforce political or religious beliefs, and building styles that have come to symbolize various philosophical schools of thought. The pyramids of Ancient Egypt were viewed as stairways to Ra, the sun god, and as such, were constant reminders to the Egyptians of the role of magic in their lives. The Greek Parthenon was based on the proportions of ideal human anatomy, and as such served as a symbol of humanism and rational thinking ("Man is the measure of all things.") The Cathedral of Notre Dame is fraught with Christian symbolism, and in the minds of many, is as powerful a relic as any saintly bone might be.

C) An example of an artistic work which inspired people to action was the Hellenistic sculpture, *Gaul Killing Himself*. This work, depicting a Gaul and his wife committing suicide rather than submitting to enslavement by the Romans, was said to have inspired Greeks and other Mediterranean peoples to resist the Roman invasions. Likewise, Michelangelo's heroic figure of *David* inspired the people of Florence to fend off stronger Italian city states and other political enemies. In more recent years, the environmentally-sensitive wrappings of the conceptual artist Christo, have focused controversy and discussion on environmental issues. As a direct result of his work, important strides in the area of soil erosion have taken place.

COMPETENCY 5.0   KNOWLEDGE OF THE VARIED AESTHETIC PRINCIPLES USED BY CULTURES IN EVALUATING ART

SKILL 5.1   Identify vocabulary used in discussing the arts.

Because the arts and humanities incorporate such a wide range of artistic fields and technical expertise, to attempt a comprehensive vocabulary list here would be futile. Instead, it may be more helpful to list vocabulary that is common to discussion of most fields in the humanities.

Any artistic endeavor has form. It occupies space and occasional, time. The concept of form is related to the overall pattern of the work, and has much to do with the artist's choice of materials and medium. The form reflects the artist's ability to work with the artistic principles of his chosen medium.

Content is an integral part of form. Content may include the subject matter of a work of art, but content implies something even deeper. It implies that the work has a meaning or a message, one that perhaps relegates the subject matter to a lower priority. Content also includes the idea of theme. Because in a work of art the form and content are inseparable, an artistic work is always a gestalt.

Subject matter and theme are closely aligned. Subject matter is the topic that is being presented, while theme deals with the underlying message that is being presented through the use of that subject matter. For example, in a historical painting of a battle scene, the subject matter may be the Battle of Gettysburg, while the theme may center around the inevitable horrors of war.

Each artistic endeavor, in any field, is an artificial device, a contrived expression of some sort. It is not reality, but is intended to convey something about reality (or fantasy) to the viewers.

Some artists strive to depict the real world in a way that is easily recognizable. This particular mode is known as realism, and is usually associated with traditional artistic forms.

Sometimes artists use reality as a springboard to other messages and ideas, distorting reality in various ways in order to express something about that reality. This is generally known as abstraction, because the artists are abstracting something of importance from recognizable objects.

Some contemporary artists by-pass reality altogether, and go directly to the message in an emotional or intellectual manner. Since no recognizable elements are used, this mode of work is referred to as non-objective.

Style is an indefinable quality about an artist's work that lends the work a sense of uniqueness. To understand style, one must learn to perceive fine distinctions between works, and be receptive to the communications of the artist.

Composition deals with the technical aspects of a work of art, specifically, how it was put together. In the visual arts, an artist uses the elements of design (line, shape, color, texture). A musician uses melody, harmony, timbre, tone, etc, while a dancer uses line, movement, timing, etc. These elements are put together into a composition by utilizing certain principles of design. In the visual arts, these principles are unity, balance, variation and repetition, to name a few. (See 5.5 for related information.) The degree of craftsmanship used in the composition is an indication of the ability or expertise of the artist.

SKILL 5.2 Discriminate among aesthetic principles of various eras and cultures.

(See 5.3 for related information.)

Although the elements of design have remained consistent throughout history, the emphasis on specific aesthetic principles has periodically shifted. Aesthetic standards or principles vary from time period to time period, and from society to society.

An obvious difference in aesthetic principles occurs between works created by eastern and western cultures. Eastern works of art are more often based on spiritual considerations, while much western art is secular in nature. In attempting to convey reality, eastern artists generally prefer to use line, local color, and a simplistic view. Western artists tend toward a literal use of line, shape, color, and texture to convey a concise, detailed, complicated view. Eastern artists portray the human figure with symbolic meanings and little regard for muscle structure, resulting in a mystical view of the human experience. Western artists use the "principle of ponderation", which requires the knowledge of both human anatomy and an expression of the human spirit.

In attempts to convey the illusion of depth or visual space in a work of art, eastern and western artists use different techniques. Eastern artists prefer a diagonal projection of eye movement into the picture plane, and often leave large areas of the surface untouched by detail. The result is the illusion of vast space, an infinite view that coincides with the spiritual philosophies of the Orient. Western artists rely on several techniques, such as overlapping planes, variation of object size, object position on the picture plane, linear and aerial perspective, color change, and various points of perspective to convey the illusion of depth. The result is space that is limited and closed.

In the application of color, eastern artists use arbitrary choices of color. Western artists generally rely on literal color usage or emotional choices of color. The end result is that eastern art tends to be more universal in nature, while western art is more individualized.

An interesting change in aesthetic principles occurred between the Renaissance period (1400-1630 A.D.) and the Baroque period (1630-1700 A.D.) in Europe. The shift is easy to understand when viewed in the light of Wolfflin's categories of stylistic development (see 5.3).

The Renaissance period was concerned with the rediscovery of the works of classical Greece and Rome. The art, literature, and architecture was inspired by classical orders, which tended to be formal, simple, and concerned with the ideal human proportions. This means that the painting, sculpture, and architecture was of a teutonic, or closed nature, composed of forms that were restrained and compact. For example, consider the visual masterpieces of the period: Raphael's painting *The School of Athens*, with its highly precisioned use of space, Michelangelo's sculpture *David*, with its compact mass, and the facade of the *Palazzo Strozzi*, with its defined use of the rectangle, arches, and rustication of the masonry.

Compare the Renaissance characteristics to those of the Baroque period. The word "baroque" means "grotesque", which was the contemporary criticism of the new style. In comparison to the styles of the Renaissance, the Baroque was concerned with the imaginative flights of human fancy. The painting, sculpture and architecture were of an ateutonic, or open nature, composed of forms that were whimsical and free-flowing. Consider again the masterpieces of the period: Ruben's painting *The Elevation of the Cross*, with it's turbulent forms of light and dark tumbling diagonally through space, Puget's sculpture *Milo of Crotona*, with it's use of open space and twisted forms, and Borromini's *Chapel of St.Ivo*, with a facade that plays convex forms against concave ones.

SKILL 5.3   Trace changes in aesthetic principles.

Although artists throughout time have used the same elements of design to compose their various artistic works, the emphasis on specific aesthetic principles has periodically shifted. Aesthetic principles vary from time period to time period, and from society to society.

In the 1920's and 30's, the German art historian, Professor Wolfflin outlined these shifts in aesthetic principles in his influential book <u>Principles of Art History</u>. He arranged these changes into five categories of "visual analysis", sometimes referred to as the "categories of stylistic development". Wolfflin was careful to point out that no style is inherently superior to any other. They are simply indicators of the phase of development of that particular time or society. However, Wolfflin goes on to state, correctly or not, that once the evolution occurs, it is impossible to regress. These modes of perception apply to drawing, painting, sculpture and architecture. They are as follows:

1. From a linear mode to a painterly mode.
This shift refers to stylistic changes that occur when perception or expression evolves from a linear form that is concerned with the contours and boundaries of objects, to perception or expression that stresses the masses and volumes of objects. From viewing objects in isolation, to seeing the relationships between objects are an important change in perception. Linear mode implies that objects are stationary and unchanging, while the painterly mode implies that objects and their relationships to other objects is always in a state of flux.

2. From plane to recession.
This shift refers to perception or expression that evolves from a planar style, when the artist views movement in the work in an "up and down" and "side to side" manner, to a recessional style, when the artist views the balance of a work in an "in and out" manner. The illusion of depth may be achieved through either style, but only the recessional style uses an angular movement forward and backward through the visual plane.

3. From closed to open form.
This shift refers to perception or expression that evolves from a sense of enclosure, or limited space, in "closed form", to a sense of freedom in "open form". The concept is obvious in architecture, as in buildings which clearly differentiate between "outside" and "inside" space, and buildings which open up the space to allow the outside to interact with the inside.

4. From multiplicity to unity.
This shift refers to an evolution from expressing unity through the use of balancing many individual parts, to expressing unity by subordinating some individual parts to others. Multiplicity stresses the balance between existing elements, whereas unity stresses emphasis, domination, and accent of some elements over other elements.

5. From absolute to relative clarity.
This shift refers to an evolution from works which clearly and thoroughly express everything there is to know about the object, to works that express only part of what there is to know, and leave the viewer to fill in the rest from his own experiences. Relative clarity, then, is a sophisticated mode, because it requires the viewer to actively participate in the "artistic dialogue". Each of the previous four categories is reflected in this, as linearity is considered to be concise while painterliness is more subject to interpretation. Planarity is more factual, while recessional movement is an illusion, and so on.

SKILL 5.4 Recognize effects of aesthetic principles on significant works of art.

(See 5.3 and 5.5 for related information.)

The Laocoon, sculpture by Hagesandros, Polydoros and Athenodoros, 2nd century A.D.

> This Hellenistic sculpture was created during the decline of ancient Greek influence. The quiet restraint of the closed forms of classical sculpture had evolved into the more dynamic, open forms of Hellenistic sculpture. The artists, although still portraying the human body as the highest ideal form, sought to capture the drama of the moment as Laocoon, the priest of Troy, is punished for his disobedience to the gods. The realistic depiction of the suffering of Laocoon and his sons is designed to evoke pity from the viewer.
>
> The aesthetic standards and principles of design (see 5.5) are apparent in this work. The curvilinear lines of the serpents and the monochromatic color of the marble serve to unify the composition. The balance is asymmetric, with Laocoon and his closest son visually balancing the other son, who is placed off to one side. The center of interest is the centrally-located head of the serpent. Eye movement and rhythm through the work follow the linear twists of the serpents and the writhing forms of the bodies. Repetition is found in the repeated loops of the serpents and the outward thrusts of the torsos as they seek to escape the grip of the snakes. Variation is present in the various sizes of the bodies, while their positioning creates negative shapes of various size and contour. Contrast is provided by the smooth finish of the torsos placed against the rougher texture of beards, hair and drapery. The space is shallow and of a planar nature, with tension created by the twist of the masses and the use of negative space.

Guernica, painting by Pablo Picasso, 1937

This abstract painting is one of the world's most powerful social commentaries, and is considered to be Picasso's most dramatic work. *Guernica* was painted as a commission for the Spanish exhibit at the Paris Exposition of 1937. Designed as a protest against man's inhumanity to man, it depicts in abstract forms the April 1937 Nazi Luftwuffe bombing of the Spanish town of Guernica, an act paid for by the Spanish Fascists who sought to destroy the source of the resistance movement in Spain. Picasso, who was prolific in a multitude of styles, including realism, chose to use abstract forms in an effort to evoke even stronger emotions against the horrors of war. The abstract forms are drawn from Christian and Spanish folk symbolism, yet the composition, like the classical art Picasso had studied just prior to this work, is closed and compact.

An analysis of the aesthetic principles shows that the work is unified by the somber black, white and gray palette, which helps to focus the viewer's attention on the message and mood. The balance is symmetrical, with forms of equal weight on either side of the canvas, and solidly built on a triangular basis. The center of interest is the centrally-located triangle of light streaming from the out-stretched lamp. Eye movement follows the horizontal format of the painting, but is occasionally broken by diagonal edges of the triangles. The rhythm is short and choppy, perhaps symbolizing the disruptive qualities of war and destruction. Repetition is evident in the repeated colors, shapes and newspaper print texture throughout the work. Variation is found in the size and positioning of the shapes, and the contrast of light and dark areas. Space is depicted on a shallow plane, with overlapping shapes providing the only illusion of depth. Tension is created by the placement of the shapes and the high contrast between lights and darks.

Number One, painting by Jackson Pollack, 1950

This non-objective work is one of Pollack's "action paintings", in which the emphasis is placed not on the finished product, but on the creative process itself. The painting was created by rolling out the canvas on the floor, then drawing in the air above the canvas in such a way that the paint would drip and splatter onto the surface. The idea is not so much to aim for a result as it is to "arrive at a statement". Action painting is also an attempt to include the elements of time and motion into the otherwise "static" arts.

The principles of design are evident in this work. The work is unified by the consistency of texture over the surface plane. The balance is symmetrical, with even visual weight on either side of the composition. The center of interest is the slightly off-center dark patch, surrounded by a lighter area. The eye movement is carried by the dark linear paint, which creates a circular pattern around the edges of the work. Repetition is evident in the use of color and manner of paint application throughout the painting. Variation is found in the contrast of lights and darks, and occasional large curves drawn in darker paint. The space was intended to be flat, but the overlapping of lines and the variation in line thickness lends the illusion of shallow depth to the work. Tension is created by the complex pattern of movement over the entire painting surface.

SKILL 5.5 Identify examples of Western and non-Western aesthetic principles.

Western Principles of design in western art include the following:

1) Unity
2) Balance
3) Center of Interest
4) Movement
5) Repetition
6) Variation
7) Rhythm
8) Contrast
9) Space
10) Tension

> These principles are apparent in artistic works throughout all historical time periods, although emphasis may shift from period to period, or from location to location, or from artist to artist.

Non-Western Around 500 A.D., Hsieh Ho, a Chinese portrait painter, composed a list of artists based on the quality of their works. He included an essay to explain his selections, and in so doing, drew up the famous "Six Principles of Hsieh Ho". These principles were so concisely written, and so well-constructed, that they became the foundation for art criticism in China.

1) The most difficult to understand, yet the most important is the principle of the "ch'i", or the force in nature that gives life to all things. It was thought that the painter must harmonize with the ch'i in order to give spirit to his work. Later, Zen mystics believed the force was within the painter himself. This energy was believed to be an essential factor in the creative process, without which a work had no form or meaning.

2) This energy was transmitted to the paper by the "bone method" or "bone-like" strength of the brushstroke. This is the confident stroke seen in both Chinese calligraphy and painting, a stroke that appears to have a clarity and life of it's own, independent of the rest of the composition.

3, 4, 5) These three principles deal mostly with representational art. They are, "conformity to the likeness of the object being represented", "correct color" ,and "thoughtful composition".

6) The sixth principle is "transmission of the tradition by making copies". This was included in order to give the painter technical expertise as well as to preserve the traditions in painting, an integral aspect of Chinese culture.

SKILL 5.6 Analyze how perceptions of popular art forms are related to perceptions of traditional art forms.

Popular art forms are generally regarded as forms of art that appeal to large numbers of people in a society, like contemporary films or even music videos. Traditional art forms are considered to be the art forms that have continued on for generations, or even centuries, such as mural painting, oil painting, marble sculpture, and the like. Understanding of popular art forms is built upon knowledge of traditional forms. The old adage "There is nothing new under the sun," appears to be true in the arts, where no idea is conceived in isolation.

Although fashion and fads are fickle, much in the arts remains constant, particularly in the realm of elements and principles of design. From Paleolithic cave drawings to Christo's wrapped buildings, art works have consisted of the same elements of line, shape, color and texture, woven together into compositions by artists who were striving to communicate with their peers or their gods. The principles of design also remain constant, although the emphasis on various principles shifts from time to time and from culture to culture. All artists must deal with balance of some sort, and contemplate the placement of their centers of interest. Some artists work with the principles in a conscious manner, while others make their decisions intuitively. The function of art as communication has remained constant, although the styles of communication mutate. In any case, understanding the how and why of various works created in the past enhances sensitivity to new works created in the present.

As society changes, and new materials and technologies progress, so, too, must art forms evolve. Because artists are often on the cutting edge of what is new in society, modern art forms are more readily accepted by a new generation of consumers, who find in them a break with the past. At the same time, the new forms may seem alien to people who are familiar with older, more traditional forms. After all, it is easier to rely on established standards by which to judge art, rather than make the effort to understand something new. It is contrary to human nature to seek change and as a result, conservative opinion lags behind.

SKILL 5.7 Justify an aesthetic preference by citing an aesthetic principle.

(See 5.4 for additional information.)

In the 1930 painting *American Gothic* by Grant Wood, the artist had to choose what kind of tool to place in the farmer's hand. The pitchfork was an excellent choice because the shape and proportions of the tines repeat the pattern and proportions found in the farmer's overalls and in the windows of the farmhouse in the background. The principle adhered to is "repetition".

In the 1784 painting *Oath of the Horatii* by David, the artist had to decide on the placement of the background arches. Because David's style was neoclassic in nature, he tended toward a formal, symmetrical balance similar to those found in the classical works of the Greeks and Romans. Therefore he divided the composition into three equal vertical sections, placing an arch in each section to frame the three groupings of people in a symmetrical fashion. The principle adhered to is "formal balance."

In the 1939 sculpture *Reclining Figure* by Henry Moore, the sculptor had to make a determination on the amount of wood to carve away from the figure. One of the factors he had to take into account was the interaction between the positive and negative shapes. (Positive shapes are often considered to be the shapes of the masses, while the negative shapes are the voids, but this is a purely relative view.) The principle adhered to is "positive/negative shape".

In the 1907 apartment house *Casa Mila* by Antonio Gaudi, the artist had to decide on the arrangement of the facade. His design eventually consisted of a series of free-form portals and balconies, arranged as close as possible to randomness found in nature. The principle adhered to is "multiplicity".

In the 1958 painting *Four Darks on Red* by Mark Rothko, the artist had to make a series of choices concerning sizes of shapes, placement of shapes, and intensity of color. These choices had to be made with regard to the visual effect Rothko sought, which was that of visual tension between the shapes. This was achieved by his strategy of placing a smaller shape on the bottom to give the illusion of instability, and surrounding that shape with a brighter intensity of red, to further isolate the shape from the others. The large dark rectangle placed on top contributes to the crushing feeling at the bottom of the painting.

COMPETENCY 6.0   **KNOWLEDGE OF INSTRUCTIONAL TECHNIQUES APPROPRIATE TO THE HUMANITIES**

SKILL 6.1   **Choose effective methods of presentation for various humanities topics.**

(See 6.2 for related information.)

Due to the very nature of the humanities, it is possible to produce creative presentation techniques for almost any humanities topic. Listed below are some suggestions.

Traditional techniques

The traditional lecture can be an effectual method of dispensing information to students, especially students who are auditory learners. For mixed learning types, lecture combined with visual notes on an overhead is a better choice. The interest level of any kind of lecture is greatly enhanced by the use of visual aids, such as posters, slides, actual artistic works or reproductions. Fortunately, the arts and humanities subject matter lends itself well to visual stimuli.

Slide shows set to music are a traditional way to introduce students to subject matter such as the works of a particular artist or style. This format works well, because after the initial presentation, the teacher can use the slides for discussion or lecture.

Field trips to galleries, museums, workshops, and other arts-related places have long served to pique the interest of students, and enable them to view first-hand works of art or historic artifacts. A visit to a band room to permit even non-musical students to try various instruments is an invaluable experience.

Guest speakers and artists-in-residence may bring to the classroom not only their expertise and enthusiasm, but also diverse points of view, an essential ingredient for a well-rounded education. For example, dance instructors who specialize in various forms of dance, such as ballet, modern jazz, or ethnic dances, may give demonstrations on different days in order for students to understand common elements in the dances as well as differing dance philosophies.

Contemporary techniques

The latest studies (and common sense!) tell educators that one of the most effective ways of helping students learn is by actively involving students right from the beginning. Less traditional, but more time-consuming methods, attempt to put this information into practice.

Student-produced videos can be created on a variety of topics, from the poetry of Shakespeare to technical information on how to develop a photographic print. Students acquire research skills, organizational skills, information on the topic, and technical skills in the field of film-making.

Role-playing by teachers is an effective technique when introducing biographical information on various historical or artistic people, such as John Locke or Vincent van Gogh. Role-playing by students ensures the retention of that information for longer periods of time. Students may be assigned roles from a single time period, such as the Renaissance, in order to convey the spirit of the times, or they may role-play a single event, such as the trial of Socrates. In order to promote comparisons and contrasts, assign roles of people throughout history who held similar and dissimilar viewpoints. An example might be for students to pose as sculptors Praxiteles, Michelangelo, Picasso, and Oldenburg, in a "meeting of the minds" to discuss their philosophies of art and the techniques used in the construction of their sculptures. Forethought and planning on the part of the teacher is the key to successful role-playing.

Art and architecture concepts lend themselves well to immediate student involvement. For example, when discussing the characteristics of mannerist painting and sculpture, have students mimic the contrived poses to help understand the artists' intentions. When discussing the function of flying buttresses, have students form two lines facing each other, with arms up and hands joined to simulate the Gothic pointed arches. Press down on the arches to show their strength. Then have two more lines of students (representing the buttresses) stand behind the others, with their hands bracing the shoulders of the students in front. Again press down on the arches, enabling students to feel the difference in support with the buttresses in place.

Having students produce models is an effective method of teaching. For example, having students assemble or construct models of famous buildings is one way to teach architectural concepts. Assigning soap carvings of the human torso to students who are studying the history of Greek sculpture is a sure way to impart an appreciation of the carving process.

Student-produced works involve students in the creative process, as well as teach technical and organizational skills, and impart information. Examples include students writing poetry, then working with, perhaps, an artist-in-residence to record the poems in a "container" of sound (literal and/or musical sounds). Students may interpret assigned literary selections verbally, then, with the help of a choreographer, express them in dance, set it to music, and record on video.

SKILL 6.2 Select effective teacher strategies for educating students of differing abilities and interests in the humanities.

(See 6.1 for related information.)

Humanities topics lend themselves admirably to lesson plans that can be informational and intriguing, educational and memorable. The key of most teaching is to find a way to interest and involve the student. Then learning takes place as a natural consequence. Many humanities instructors find an interdisciplinary approach to be a most effective way to hold student interest as well as convey significant concepts. Strategies listed below are general ones, easily adapted and combined in many ways.

1.) Individual analysis of readings/materials.

2.) Group analysis of readings/materials.

3.) Traditional lecture/class discussion.

4.) Role-playing by teacher, with costumes, props, examples of work by various artists, musicians, authors, philosophers, etc.

5.) Role-playing by students, with examples of work by various artists, musicians, authors, philosophers, etc. May be individual or in a panel, such as a "Meeting of the Minds" discussion, or may be a class simulation, with everyone filling a role.

6.) Co-operative learning in pairs or small groups. May utilize packets, resource materials, flash cards, etc.

7.) Listening to various music samples as a group, followed by group discussion.

8.) Viewing music/slide show of examples of art, followed by group discussion.

9.) Viewing educational films of assorted humanities topics.

10.) Individual, group, or class production of an original work of art, ie. dance, music, painting, sculpture, architectural model, poetry, story, etc.

11.) Individual, group, or class production of a duplicated work of art in any field. (Especially helpful in attempting to trace the evolution of a particular style.)

12.) Individual, group, or class production of original work combining two or more art forms, ie, recording poetry with musical accompaniment, poetry and dance, art and music, etc. (Using a traditional or historical source as a starting point is often helpful, such as students interpreting, in dance, scenes from *Beowulf*.)

13.) Class field trips to local art museums, galleries, playhouses, businesses related to the arts, ie. photography studios, framing stores, etc.

14.) Guest-speakers in any number of humanities disciplines, hopefully bringing tangible "props" with them in addition to information.

15.) Artist-in-residence guests can be extremely helpful, not only in serving as guest-speakers, but in helping students produce works of art. Artists-in-residence generally serve a residency of two to four weeks, routinely appearing in the school in several capacities, but primarily as producing a work at the school.

SKILL 6.3 Select appropriate evaluation methods for assessing and measuring student responses in humanities classes.

Evaluation methods for humanities courses should be varied in order to insure an adequate base for evaluation. The methods should be appropriate to the abilities of the students being tested, as well as the subject and skills being evaluated.

List of Possible Evaluation Techniques

Written tests such as essay or discussion questions, or research papers, are an appropriate method for evaluating writing skills, critical thinking skills, information retention, and research skills.

Multiple choice tests appear to work well for evaluating retention of specific information.
Oral tests can be used in creative ways to evaluate many skills, including information retention, critical thinking skills, and progress of appreciation for the arts.
Hands-on projects, activities, and creative work such as student-produced dance, painting, poetry, etc., is an excellent way to gauge progress of technical techniques, as well as enhance appreciation of an art form. Creativity, as well as critical thinking skills are encouraged, as well as evaluated.

Group evaluation works well for projects that entail students working with other students. It is advantageous to discuss the standards for evaluation before the testing, and even better to have the students themselves compose the standards to be used.
Peer grading in addition to teacher grading is also advantageous in this situation.

Peer evaluation is an effective technique for learning, as well as for evaluating. It is especially effective when students themselves draw up the standards for evaluation before grading begins. It works well with short written work, and hands-on projects.

SKILL 6.4 Determine appropriate and useful academic and community resources available to humanities students.

Each community has unique sources for cultural enrichment. Included below is a generic listing of places to begin the search for people and organizations that can help in the educational process.

Local schools and universities may provide a rich assortment of teachers and professors who might serve as guest speakers or consultants.

Local museums and galleries may provide not only people with expertise in the arts, but also educational materials, such as posters, slides, books, or videos. The real resource of these institutions is in their various collections, which may be utilized through field trips.

Private schools that teach art, dance, theater, and the like are often willing to coordinate with public schools. The instructors in these schools can often provide short, temporary expertise for special projects, or often will serve as consultants on special projects. (Working in public schools also broadens the client base they may draw from.)

Local businesses that are associated with the arts, such as publishers, designers, framers, dance outfitters, etc. are often willing to share their expertise with students. (Again, this helps them to broaden their client base.) Organizations such as art leagues, poetry circles, community theater groups, and historical societies are a treasure trove of people who love to assist students in many ways, such as providing educational instruction, money for scholarships, or even supplies for worthy, needy students or classrooms.

Practicing artists of all kinds can be found in community organizations, such as those listed above, galleries, craft shows, and even in the yellow pages! They often times make excellent guest speakers and may even work as artists-in-residence, either independently or through an arts organization.

Sample Test

Directions: Read each item and choose the best response for each.

1. **The principle which is not used in architecture is**

   A. proportion

   B. space

   C. balance

   D. time

2. **The genre of Handel's *Messiah* is**

   A. oratorio

   B. overture

   C. sonata

   D. suite

3. **In the visual arts, a genre may refer to**

   A. scenes of everyday life

   B. a type of tempra paint

   C. the choice of medium

   D. opera

4. **A musical work written for one or more solo instruments with accompaniment by an orchestra is a**

   A. cantata

   B. symphony

   C. concerto

   D. sonata

5. **Plato's *Republic* centers on a discussion of**

   A. the ideal society

   B. Athenian history

   C. the teachings of Socrates

   D. a justification of politics

6. **The Greek philosopher who believed that only change is real, and that the universe is in a state of flux was**

   A. Epicurus

   B. Heraclitus

   C. Socrates

   D. Cicero

7. The Renaissance author of The Prince was

   A. Dante

   B. Machiavelli

   C. Mirandola

   D. Salutati

8. Stoicism is a philosophy based on the idea that

   A. reason can overcome suffering

   B. the universe is mechanical

   C. knowledge is limited, so nothing can be proven

   D. all spiritual things emanate from God

9. The founder of existentialism was

   A. Hegel

   B. Russell

   C. Sartre

   D. Kant

10. Sympathetic magic is usually associated with this style of art.

    A. Primitive

    B. Christian

    C. Rococo

    D. Impressionism

11. Classicism in music and literature

    A. was designed to appeal to the masses

    B. originated in the medieval period in Europe

    C. was based on linear perspective

    D. was formal, quiet and restrained.

12. The Epic of Gilgamesh originated with this culture.

    A. Babylonian

    B. Greek

    C. Japanese

    D. Byzantine

13. The elongation of the human figure in Byzantine religious art, referred to as the hieratic style, represented

    A. spirituality

    B. original sin

    C. forgiveness

    D. a characteristic of the mosaic technique.

14. Romanesque architecture is not known for it's

    A. thick walls

    B. clerestory windows

    C. flying buttresses

    D. dark interiors

15. A pendentive is a

    A. medieval troubadour

    B. genre of literature

    C. melancholic piece of music

    D. triangle of masonry

16. The guiding principle of the Italian Renaissance was

    A. Humanism

    B. Mannerism

    C. Neoclassicism

    D. Sfumato

17. During the Renaissance, these two Christian humanists advocated a return to the teachings of Jesus.

    A. Machiavelli and Castiglione

    B. Erasmus and More

    C. Dante and Mirandola

    D. Petrarch and Bruni

18. Engravings and oil painting originated in this country.

    A. Italy

    B. Japan

    C. Germany

    D. Flanders

19. A characteristic of Baroque art is

    A. use of chiaroscuro

    B. simplicity of line

    C. cubism

    D. small scale

20. A characteristic that does not apply to a fugue is

    A. ornamentation

    B. dramatic shifts

    C. large scale performances

    D. powerful lyrics

21. Shakespeare's plays often focused on

    A. everyday situations

    B. human psychology

    C. religious values

    D. ancient mythology

22. The philosopher of the Enlightenment who was a champion of civil liberties was

    A. Hume

    B. Bentham

    C. Descartes

    D. Voltaire

23. The famous Greek sculptor known for the Cnidian Aphrodite was

    A. Myron

    B. Polyclitus

    C. Praxiteles

    D. Heraclitus

24. The Flemish artist who created the painting entitled The Arnolfini Marriage was

    A. Jan van Eyck

    B. Hugh van der Goes

    C. Bosch

    D. Durer

25. A characteristic of Rococo architecture and interior design was

    A. shell-like ornamentation

    B. dark marble floors

    C. heavy stone tracery

    D. scale based on human proportions

26. The Humanitarian painting style of the 18th century was characterized by

    A. strong diagonal compositions

    B. realistic portrayal of human proportions

    C. social commentary

    D. delight in romantic love

27. Emotion in romantic music is suggested by

   A. the five-tone scale

   B. key changes and dissonance

   C. contrapuntal mode

   D. strong percussion

28. Dickens and Balzac created works that reflected this style.

   A. Romantic

   B. Gothic

   C. Victorian

   D. Realistic

29. Impressionism in art and music was an attempt to

   A. capture the transitory aspects of the world

   B. impress the audience with a photographic-like view of the world

   C. express heart-felt emotions about nature

   D. portray the common people in a heroic light

30. The German art, literature and film-making style that sought strong emotional response was

   A. Cubism

   B. Dadaism

   C. Expressionism

   D. Photo-realism

31. A central difference between abstract art and non-objective art is that

   A. abstract art contains real subject matter

   B. abstract art has more structure

   C. non-objective art is organized by strict adherence to form

   D. non-objective art is aimed at the subliminal level of brain activity

32. Characteristics of a formal essay do not include

   A. concise structure

   B. reliance on logic

   C. personal attitude

   D. evidence to convince the reader

33. The Greek philosopher known for his exchange and analysis of opinions was

   A. Socrates

   B. Plato

   C. Aristotle

   D. Diogenes

34. The philosopher who coined this well-known phrase "I think, therefore I am" was

   A. Bacon

   B. St. Augustine

   C. Descartes

   D. Locke

35. The year that marks the official collapse of the Roman Empire was

   A. 380 B.C.

   B. 476 A.D.

   C. 500 A.D.

   D. 1500 A.D.

36. The Peloponnesian Wars in Greece took place before the Greco-Persian Wars.

   A. True

   B. False

37. The Code of Hammurabi was developed by this civilization.

   A. Sumerians

   B. Babylonians

   C. Greeks

   D. Romans

38. The great Roman poet Virgil was influenced by the writings of Marcus Aurelius.

   A. True

   B. False

39. Dante wrote the Divine Comedy before the first wave of the Bubonic Plague hit Europe.

   A. True

   B. False

40. The French Revolutionary War was inspired, in part, by the success of the American Revolution.

   A. True

   B. False

41. Which pair of authors did not write during the same historical period?

   A. Marx and Dickens

   B. Locke and Diderot

   C. Sartre and Hegel

   D. Machiavelli and Shakespeare

42. Which philosophical idea is not associated with the ancient Greeks?

   A. Reason is a superior approach to decision-making

   B. man is capable of governing himself

   C. man should strive toward perfection

   D. man is an inferior creature created by an uncaring god

43. Much of the doctrine of the medieval Roman Catholic Church, including the belief that it was the duty of the Church to find and punish heretics, was derived from the writings of this influential author.

   A. St. Boethius

   B. St. Aquinas

   C. St. Augustine

   D. St. Joan

44. This statement is not a tenet of Humanism.

   A. classical models of art should serve as inspiration to strive for perfection

   B. man's highest goal should be to serve god

   C. man's highest goal should be to "acquire excellence"

   D. it is man's ability to reason that gives him a unique place in the world

45. The philosophes of the Enlightenment concerned themselves with the issues of

   A. individual rights and the responsibility of government to provide them

   B. methodology of the scientific revolution

   C. responsibility of industry toward the proletariat

   D. distribution of wealth in an ideal society

46. This philosophical idea is not associated with the views of Karl Marx.

    A. Social evolution is inevitable

    B. Proletarians will eventually overthrow all governments

    C. In a communistic society, the government will eventually wither away

    D. Capitalism is the most advanced economic order

47. The Neolithic revolution was

    A. war between Neanderthals and Cro-Magnon men

    B. shift in economics from food-hunting to food-producing

    C. a shift from old-stone age weapons to new-stone age weapons

    D. a shift from new-stone age weapons to the bronze age

48. A theocracy is government by

    A. the elite

    B. the people

    C. theory

    D. religion

49. The social structure of Europe during the Middle Ages was based on

    A. the manorial system

    B. mercantilism

    C. communism

    D. feudalism

50. A constitutional monarchy is a government in which

    A. the power of the monarch is limited by law

    B. the monarch is appointed by a law-making body

    C. the monarch has no power

    D. the monarch has unlimited power

51. The influence of China on western culture can best be viewed in the field of

    A. architecture

    B. religion

    C. film-making

    D. language

52. The influence of Russia on western arts can best be viewed in the field of

   A. ballet

   B. painting

   C. film-making

   D. opera

53. In the religion of Hinduism, the three aspects of the God-head are

   A. Brahma, Vishnu, and Shiva

   B. Nirvana, Vishnu, and Buddha

   C. Veda, Ramayana, and Buddha

   D. Rig-Veda, Rama, and Shiva

54. The philosophy best associated with Lao-tse is

   A. government should be a strong force in society

   B. mankind should live in fear of the gods

   C. mankind should live in harmony with nature

   D. mankind should strive toward intellectual perfection

55. The Japanese religion of Zen Buddhism emphasizes

   A. belief in reincarnation

   B. adherence to the caste system

   C. ancestor worship

   D. spirituality through meditation

56. Major contributions of the Moslems to western culture occurred the field of

   A. religion

   B. language

   C. engineering

   D. medicine

57. The most significant contribution from Greco-Roman civilizations is the belief in

   A. Stoic philosophy

   B. practical architecture

   C. the possibilities of democratic governments

   D. justice by law and order

58. The contribution to western civilization not associated with Judaism is the

   A. belief in ethical treatment of others

   B. belief in polytheism

   C. belief in monotheism

   D. belief in the supremacy of law

59. The great literary achievement of the Hebrew people is the

   A. Upanishads

   B. Rig-Veda

   C. Old Testament

   D. New Testament

60. The main contribution of Christianity to western civilization is the

   A. advocating of ethical treatment of others

   B. belief in saints

   C. spirituality found in church art and architecture

   D. transmission of Hebraic history

61. Geography affects the development of mankind by

   A. dictating which resources man has available to him

   B. affecting the genetic material of mankind, thus speeding or slowing evolution

   C. providing obstacles for man to overcome

   D. broadening human horizons

62. The influence of geography on early societies is most apparent in the field of

   A. art

   B. early government

   C. weapon construction

   D. religious beliefs

63. Universal themes are those which

   A. explain how the universe was created

   B. explain the nature of the universe

   C. can be experienced by all people

   D. belong to specific groups of people

64. The dominant themes in Egyptian culture center around

   A. belief in the ideal human form

   B. preparation for the afterlife

   C. obedience to the law

   D. fertility rites

65. The dominant themes in sculpture from the Roman period include

   A. realism and glorification of the state

   B. idealism and law

   C. religious values and politics

   D. mythology and divinity of rulers

66. Characteristics of Baroque art and literature include

   A. subject matter centered around mythology and social commentary

   B. use of drama and psychology

   C. miniature scale and social commentary

   D. realism and history

67. Neo-classic themes during the 18th century centered on

   A. rights of the individual

   B. virtue and heroism

   C. artifice and whimsy

   D. grandeur and splendor

68. Twentieth century themes are marked by

   A. practicality

   B. idealism

   C. realism

   D. diversity

69. In twentieth century architecture, the hallmark is

   A. "form follows function"

   B. "man is the measure of all things"

   C. use of natural materials

   D. "picturesque"

70. History plays a role in the humanities by

    A. providing undisputed factual material

    B. providing a common frame of reference for human experiences

    C. providing rich sources of unbiased opinions

    D. discouraging originality in thinking because all ideas are based on ones that came before

71. The field of Russian literature is marked by

    A. authors who wrote brilliant intellectual theses

    B. authors who documented social ills

    C. stories of fantasy and wit

    D. stories based on folk lore

72. The 1937 painting Guernica by Picasso is an example of

    A. historical influence in the humanities

    B. non-objective painting

    C. a painting with the emphasis on color tension

    D. realism

73. The following is not an example of a thematic motif in realistic art.

    A. Last Judgment

    B. Buddha

    C. Color

    D. The Storming of the Bastille

74. Religious symbols used to portray the theme of the Annunciation are the

    A. dove, lily, and closed book

    B. emanating rays, rainbow and goat

    C. Star of Bethlehem, keys and closed book

    D. emanating rays, keys and angels

75. Michelangelo's sculpture of David depicts the hero in the stance of

    A. hurling the rock

    B. contemplating Goliath

    C. holding Goliath's head

    D. receiving praise after the kill

76. This artist is not known for utilizing the theme of marriage in his works.

    A. Hogarth

    B. Mozart

    C. van Eyck

    D. Debussy

77. These two factors contributed greatly to the decline of illiteracy in Renaissance Europe.

    A. the Reformation and the Inquisition

    B. the printing press and vernacular writing

    C. the dictionary and encyclopedia

    D. the Scientific Revolution and the Enlightenment

78. Impressionism benefited from the scientific studies of light and the

    A. advancements in eye surgery

    B. industrial revolution

    C. new synthetic paints

    D. new gas lighting in theaters

79. During the 1800's, musicians were able to produce more uniform sounds due to the

    A. mass production of printed music

    B. standardization in the production of musical instruments

    C. new metallic alloys discovered

    D. increased frequency of traveling conductors

80. Twentieth century architecture was significantly affected by the

    A. production of structural steel

    B. tendency toward "open plans"

    C. ability to control interior climate

    D. rise in property costs

81. Two styles of art which focus on light and a specific moment of time are

    A. Renaissance and Baroque

    B. Baroque and Neoclassism

    C. Neoclassism and Romanticism

    D. Baroque and Impressionism

82. Impressionism in art and music have in common these attributes.

    A. location and technology

    B. mood and reflection of light

    C. time period and technology

    D. contrasting color and timing

83. Raphael was profoundly influenced by this work early in his career.

    A. Caravaggio's Calling of St. Matthew

    B. Mirandola's Oration on the Dignity of Man

    C. Michelangelo's Sistine ceiling

    D. Cervantes' Don Quixote

84. The visual artist not known for his "spotlight" technique is

    A. Caravaggio

    B. Rubens

    C. Rembrandt

    D. Renoir

85. Impressionistic art is based on the

    A. blending of complimentary colors in the eye

    B. impasto technique of painting

    C. expression of the artist's anger

    D. beauty of nature

86. The equivalent of impressionism in philosophy may be summed up in this statement.

    A. "Man is the measure of all things."

    B. "The universe is in a constant state of flux."

    C. "Man's greatest good is service to the state."

    D. "Man has a right to dissolve governments if they become tyrannical."

87. Dante's Divine Comedy was not an inspiration for this creator.

    A. Eugene Delacroix

    B. Victor Hugo

    C. Franz Liszt

    D. St. Augustine

88. This twentieth century author was noticeably influenced by Homer's Odyssey.

   A. Ernest Hemingway

   B. J.D.Salinger

   C. James Joyce

   D. George Orwell

89. This composer is associated with the musical form of the fugue.

   A. Hayden

   B. Beethoven

   C. Bach

   D. Brahms

90. This architect is associated with the International Style.

   A. van der Rohe

   B. Frank Lloyd Wright

   C. Le Corbusier

   D. I.M. Pei

91. The master of spectacle in the field of opera was

   A. Wagner

   B. Puccini

   C. Mozart

   D. Vivaldi

92. Associated with the concept of surrealism, this artist is known for his "mind scapes".

   A. de Kooning

   B. Miro

   C. Braque

   D. Dali

93. After the Russian Revolution of 1917, the Communist Party persecuted authors who dared to express views contrary to party doctrine. This is an example of

   A. a social constraint on the arts

   B. a religious constraint on the arts

   C. an economic constraint on the arts

   D. a political constraint on the arts

94. In 1830, Charles X of France attempted to exert political constraint on intellectual freedom by

   A. burning books

   B. censoring scientific journals

   C. censoring the press

   D. exiling engineers

95. In 399 B.C., Socrates was condemned to death on trumped up charges of corrupting the youth of Athens. His farewell oratory to the Athenians was recorded by

   A. Aristotle

   B. Plato

   C. Sophocles

   D. Aristagorus

96. An example of a religious constraint on intellectual freedom was the

   A. U.S.Congress 1990's withdrawal of grant money to homosexual artists

   B. 1564 Council of Trent listing of prohibited books

   C. Spartan refusal to acknowledge achievements in the arts

   D. Athenian sentencing of Socrates to death by hemlock

97. The art of primitive societies is often filled with images of animals. This is probably due to the primitive belief in

   A. conservation

   B. environmental awareness

   C. sympathetic magic

   D. worship of nature gods

98. Which is not an example of a religious convention in the arts?

   A. No human imagery is permitted in Islamic art

   B. Egyptian pharaohs were always depicted as deities

   C. St. Joan is depicted with armor

   D. Byzantine crucifixes emphasized the suffering of Jesus

99. The Romans portrayed historical events by

   A. using a biased view from only the Roman standpoint

   B. enlisting the aid of the most objective historians

   C. writing epic poems stemming from an oral tradition

   D. relying on sacred texts for details

100. Preliterate societies preserved history through the use of

   A. storytellers

   B. mnemonic devises

   C. drawings

   D. all of these

101. During the medieval period in Europe, the Roman Catholic Church served as a state government, even to the point of

   A. collecting taxes

   B. waging war

   C. enforcing laws

   D. all of these

102. The Winged Victory of Samothrace was founded on the philosophical concept of

   A. existentialism

   B. stoicism

   C. idealism

   D. skepticism

103. Delacroix's painting <u>Liberty Leading the People</u> is founded on the philosophical premise of

   A. Nietzsche's view that mankind could evolve into a species of "supermen"

   B. Marxist view that the proletariat will eventually overthrow all government

   C. Hegel's view that only in government can mankind find freedom from disorder

   D. Bentham's view that government should provide the greatest good for the greatest number

104. Opinions concerning the role of humans in the universe may be contemplated in the works of

   A. the ancient Greeks and Romans

   B. artists, authors, and philosophers from every time period and culture

   C. philosophy texts only

   D. religious texts only

105. Medieval art works remained anonymous in order for artists to

   A. avoid unwanted recognition

   B. avoid unwanted criticism

   C. avoid the sin of pride

   D. avoid embarrassment over their illiteracy

106. Medieval architecture mirrored the belief in God's supremacy over mankind with the symbolism found in it's

   A. spires

   B. stained glass

   C. depictions of hell

   D. all of these

107. The Protestant Reformation gained popularity, largely due to

   A. the vernacular translation of the Bible

   B. the invention of the printing press

   C. the excessive wealth of the Church

   D. the writings of Renaissance humanist authors

108. The absurdist plays of Jean-Paul Sartre reflect the philosophy that

   A. mankind is incapable of forming his own future

   B. mankind is incapable of self-government

   C. human freedom leads only to terror

   D. God is existent in all living things

109. The Dadaist Movement was based on the radical idea of

   A. art to reflect the death of art

   B. Nietzsche's "superman" theory

   C. the relativity of time

   D. the possibility of alien visits to the earth

110. A film is created, depicting the life of a composer who, feeling abandoned by God, plots to take the life of a younger, brilliant composer who he thinks God is favoring. The universal theme is

   A. Man vs. God

   B. Man vs. Man

   C. Good vs. Bad

   D. Man vs. Society

111. The role of dance in a society is an indicator of attitudes toward gender.

    A. True

    B. False

112. An example of how cultural attitudes toward gender are reflected in the arts can be best viewed in the literature of

    A. Edgar Allen Poe

    B. Jules Verne

    C. Virginia Woolf

    D. Tennessee Williams

113. The pyramids of ancient Egypt are thought to have been a visual manifestation of the religious concept of

    A. a ray of the Sun God, fallen from the sky

    B. a stairway to heaven

    C. a container for spiritual energy

    D. the God-head

114. The contemporary conceptual art of Christo lends itself to the contemplation of

    A. human idealism

    B. social ills of industrial nations

    C. environmental issues

    D. religious values

115. The Hellenistic sculpture Gaul Killing Himself, was conceived in order to

    A. honor the Gauls who were resisting Roman seizure of land

    B. chide the Greeks for not resisting the Romans

    C. advocate the use of suicide in extreme situations

    D. portray a realistic subject

116. In the arts, content and form are inseparable. This relationship is referred to by the psychological term of

    A. Bonding

    B. Gestalt

    C. Zeitgeist

    D. Schizophrenia

117. An obvious difference between eastern and western aesthetic standards appears in the treatment of

   A. perspective

   B. shading

   C. linear drawing

   D. texture

118. The following shift is not included in Wolfflin's categories of visual analysis.

   A. linear to painterly

   B. closed to open

   C. dark to light

   D. absolute to relative clarity

119. "Aesthetics" deals with

   A. subject matter

   B. theme

   C. quality of materials

   D. the nature of beauty

120. In a middle school level humanities class, the most appropriate activity for students learning about Greek drama would be to

   A. memorize the Greek alphabet

   B. memorize lines from Oedipus Rex

   C. construct masks of dramatic types

   D. watch a film of a Greek play

121. In a high school humanities class, the most effective method for teaching architectural principles is to

   A. invite an architect to speak to the class

   B. take students on a field trip to the drafting room

   C. arrange for students to construct models of the principles

   D. give a traditional lecture with slides

122. In selecting the most appropriate method of assessing students who have just completed on unit on dance, the best choice would be

   A. written essay

   B. journal entry

   C. multiple choice test

   D. hands-on activity

123. The most appropriate place to locate an artist-in-residence would be

   A. universities

   B. art organizations

   C. word of mouth

   D. museums

124. Which of the following is not an effective contemporary technique for presenting topics in the humanities?

   A. Student-produced videos

   B. Role-playing by students

   C. Work sheets

   D. Role-playing by teachers

125. Student-produced works are effective learning tools because they

   A. involve the creative process

   B. teach organizational skills

   C. impart information

   D. all of these

Answer Key

1.	D	26.	C	51.	B	76.	D	101.	C
2.	A	27.	B	52.	A	77.	B	102.	C
3.	A	28.	D	53.	A	78.	C	103.	B
4.	C	29.	A	54.	C	79.	B	104.	C
5.	A	30.	C	55.	D	80.	A	105.	D
6.	B	31.	A	56.	D	81.	D	106.	B
7.	B	32.	C	57.	C	82.	B	107.	C
8.	A	33.	B	58.	B	83.	C	108.	A
9.	C	34.	B	59.	C	84.	D	109.	A
10.	A	35.	B	60.	A	85.	A	110.	A
11.	D	36.	B	61.	B	86.	B	111.	C
12.	A	37.	A	62.	D	87.	D	112.	B
13.	A	38.	A	63.	C	88.	C	113.	C
14.	C	39.	C	64.	B	89.	C	114.	A
15.	D	40.	D	65.	A	90.	A	115.	B
16.	A	41.	C	66.	B	91.	A	116.	A
17.	B	42.	D	67.	B	92.	D	117.	C
18.	D	43.	C	68.	D	93.	D	118.	C
19.	A	44.	B	69.	A	94.	C	119.	D
20.	D	45.	A	70.	B	95.	B	120.	C
21.	B	46.	D	71.	B	96.	B	121.	C
22.	D	47.	B	72.	A	97.	C	122.	D
23.	C	48.	D	73.	C	98.	C	123.	B
24.	A	49.	C	74.	A	99.	A	124.	C
25.	A	50.	A	75.	B	100.	D	125.	D

XAMonline, INC. 21 Orient Ave. Melrose, MA 02176
Toll Free number 800-509-4128
TO ORDER Fax 781-662-9268 OR www.XAMonline.com

FLORIDA TEACHER CERTIFICATION EXAMINATIONS - FTCE - 2008

PO#   Store/School:

Bill to Address 1   Ship to address

City, State Zip

Credit card number _____-_____-_____-_____   expiration_____

EMAIL _____

PHONE   **FAX**

13# ISBN 2007	TITLE	Qty	Retail	Total
978-1-58197-900-8	Art Sample Test K-12			
978-1-58197-689-2	Biology 6-12			
978-1-58197-046-3	Chemistry 6-12			
978-1-58197-047-0	Earth/Space Science 6-12			
978-1-58197-578-9	Educational Media Specialist PK-12			
978-1-58197-347-1	Elementary Education K-6			
978-1-58197-292-4	English 6-12			
978-1-58197-274-0	Exceptional Student Ed. K-12			
978-1-58197-294-8	FELE Florida Ed. Leadership			
978-1-58197-619-9	French Sample Test 6-12			
978-1-58197-615-1	General Knowledge			
978-1-58197-586-4	Guidance and Counseling PK-12			
978-1-58197-045-6	Humanities K-12			
978-1-58197-640-3	Mathematics 6-12			
978-1-58197-597-0	Middle Grades English 5-9			
978-1-58197-662-5	Middle Grades General Science 5-9			
978-1-58197-286-3	Middle Grades Integrated Curriculum			
978-1-58197-284-9	Middle Grades Math 5-9			
978-1-58197-590-1	Middle Grades Social Science 5-9			
978-1-58197-616-8	Physical Education K-12			
978-1-58197-044-9	Physics 6-12			
978-1-58197-657-1	Prekindergarten/Primary PK-3			
978-1-58197-695-3	Professional Educator			
978-1-58197-659-5	Reading K-12			
978-1-58197-270-2	Social Science 6-12			
978-1-58197-583-3	Spanish K-12			
			SUBTOTAL	
p/handling $8.25 one title, $11.00 two titles, $15.00 three or more titles				
			TOTAL